Fear Free,
Faith Filled

Fear Free,
Faith Filled

by
Marilyn Hickey

HARRISON HOUSE
Tulsa, Oklahoma

Unless otherwise indicated,
all Scripture quotations are taken from
the *King James Version* of the Bible.

Fear Free, Faith Filled
ISBN 0-89274-259-3
Copyright © 1982 by Marilyn Hickey Ministries
P. O. Box 10606
Denver, Colorado 80210

Published by Harrison House, Inc.
P. O. Box 35035
Tulsa, Oklahoma 74135

Contents

1

What Is Fear?

But without faith it is impossible to please him (God) (Heb. 11:6).

Fear is the opposite of faith. We are either in faith or in fear: the two cannot exist in the same place at the same time. **Fear is Satan's number one weapon against the Christian.** Through the Word of God, you can banish fear from your life!

Put your hand on your heart and pray this prayer:

Father, I thank You for Your wonderful Word which is Spirit and life to me.

I thank You that the Word sets me free. I thank You for the anointing that

**resides upon me and in me to set me free
from the bondage of fear.**

**In Jesus' name,
Amen.**

Definition of Fear

The Greek word for fear is *phobos*. It
is the word from which we get our
English word *phobia*. Fear is a phobia
which becomes more intense as you
think on it, feed on it, and become more
involved in it.

Phobos means "flight, dread, or
terror." A person who has a phobia
tends to be nervous and flighty in his
reactions. He dreads facing certain
things and is terrified by the object of
his fear or phobia.

Another Greek word for fear is *deilia,*
the fearfulness that the Apostle Paul
speaks of in 2 Timothy 1:7 when he
declares: *For God hath not given us the
spirit of fear; but of power, and of love, and
of a sound mind*. This kind of fear is never
used in a positive sense because it
denotes cowardliness and timidity.

Yet another word for fear in Greek is *eulabeia* which means "caution." It can also mean "reverence." We use it when speaking of the fear that is in love and, conversely, the love that is in fear. It also has to do with the fear of our heavenly Father. We are cautious in the way we obey Him and in the way we do His work.

Have you ever felt yourself shaking inside because you were afraid of a certain situation? That kind of fear is *entromos*, which means "trembling with fear."

Fearlessness

The best word of all that has to do with fear is *aphobos*. This word means "without fear." One of the places it is found in the Bible is in Luke 1:74: *That he would grant unto us, that we being delivered out of the hand of our enemies might serve him without fear.*

Aphobos implies "being without fear among the Lord's people as the Lord's servant." At times, we can be fearful of other Christians and their opinions of us—of what we do or don't do. You can imagine all the opinions we get in the ministry about what we are supposed to do and not supposed to do.

People frequently "feel led" to tell me what I should do in a particular situation. Sometimes there will be fifteen such opinions offered to me—all different and all "from the Lord." You have to reach the place that your priorities are in following the Lord and His Word, regardless of whether or not you are pleasing to people.

If you are a leader of a Sunday School class or some other group, you must follow Jesus and stand uncompromisingly on God's Word. If you get involved in what other Christians think, you can really have problems.

Years ago a young girl in our church died of leukemia. This was a shock because we had prayed and stood in faith for her healing. When she died, it was nerve-racking for all of us.

A woman from outside the church called every family in the church and said, "Now, if the pastors are **really** spiritual, they will go to the funeral and raise that girl from the dead. If they don't do this, you can see that they don't really believe the Word. But I'll be there, and I'll raise her from the dead."

This woman was not a member of any church, nor was she addicted to the Word—and she had a flaky background to begin with. Through her calls, she was sowing discord in the church.

The night before the funeral, I had at least ten telephone calls. I was home alone at the time because my husband was out of town. Each of the people who called told me what the Lord was supposedly telling them that my husband was to do at the funeral. I never heard so many different opinions in my life! To be honest, I was afraid of what would happen at the funeral with all the confusion from the outside.

When my husband came home, I told him about all the phone calls I had been receiving. As I related the story to him, I became very distraught.

"What's wrong with you?" he asked. "We're looking to God. Lots of unsaved young people will be coming to that funeral tomorrow, and I'm claiming souls for Jesus. There's not going to be any confusion because we're taking power and authority over the Devil tonight. He isn't going to do anything!"

Later, that woman even got in touch with the family of the girl while they were in great grief and distress. She also tried to cause some confusion with them the morning of the funeral.

My husband Wally met her outside the church and told her, "If you come in and try anything out of line, I'll have the police there to sit you down."

If we had looked at all the circumstances, we would have been afraid of Christians! But we took power and authority over the enemy and went to the funeral.

The anointing of God moved in that service. Many young people indicated that they had received Jesus Christ as their personal Savior. We can always minister without being afraid of the opinions of others if we are moving in the Word.

There is another scripture, Philippians 1:14, in which the word *aphobos* is used: *And many of the brethren in the Lord, waxing confident by my bonds, are much more bold to speak the word without fear.*

This means that you need not be afraid of how a person is going to react when you teach the Word, minister the Word, or share it on a personal basis. You can have confidence that the Word will not return void. (Is. 55:11.) It *will* come to pass!

Once when I was teaching a group of Mormons, the enemy tried to put a fear on me. I wasn't so afraid of the

Mormons as I was concerned that they wouldn't receive the Word. The last morning of the retreat, they all prayed the sinner's prayer and accepted the Lord Jesus Christ.

Immediately, the enemy said to me, "Yes, but they probably didn't mean it. You just gave them a high-powered sales job, and they did it to please you!"

When I was teaching in Duluth, a couple came up to me the last Sunday night I was there and said, "Marilyn, we are Mormons. A very good friend of ours who was at the Mormon retreat told us of the changes in those women's lives after they had prayed with you."

Isn't it good that God lets us hear some of these things? It makes us want to slap the Devil in the face!

Jude 12 tells us not to be afraid of evil or false shepherds. The Devil will recount to you such stories as that of the People's Temple in Guyana, South America. Evil spirits deceived the members of that group into taking their own lives under the leadership of the false shepherd, Jim Jones. You can understand how the enemy will try to strike fear in you by saying, ''You know, you could get off into something false and evil.'' But remember, God says that we are not to be afraid of false or evil shepherds. God can, and will, deal with them.

An excellent scripture in Proverbs tells us how to keep ourselves free from fear: *Whoso hearkeneth unto me shall dwell safely, and shall be quiet from fear of evil* (Prov. 1:33).

If you will hear God's Word (because the Word is His voice), and listen to what God is saying, you will be quiet from fear of evil and will dwell in a safe place. Keeping your ears tuned to the Word keeps you out of the realm of fear. I don't mean reading the Word a couple of times a week, but feeding on it every day. It will bring peace to your spirit.

Attendant Fear

Let's examine the Old Testament definition of fear. Basically it comes from the Hebrew word *pachad*, which means "to tremble, to be on guard or in terror." It also means "an attendant, a life companion."

Do you realize that the Bible says that we were under the bondage of fear all our lives? *And deliver them who through fear of death were all their lifetime subject to bondage* (Heb. 2:15).

The Old Testament word for fear means "a lifetime companion." Hebrews 2 says that all your life you had a companion—fear—until you came to Jesus and let Him set you free from this life-long companion. Jesus names what kind of fear it was: the fear of death. Jesus knew this was the lifetime companion of bondage.

There is an attendant, a fear, born in babies. As our children grow up, we feed them more fear by saying things like, "Be careful, honey, you're going to fall,'' or, ''Don't cross the street alone; a car might run over you.'' When they learn to ride a bicycle, we tell them, ''Be careful. There are lots of accidents on bicycles. Be sure to watch out for cars!''

When they begin school, we say, ''Now, the first day may really be hard on you. The kids may not like you. Someone may knock you down, but you will be all right.''

Do you see how we begin to build on that in-born fear and help it to develop? I don't care to have that kind of life-time companion. Do you?

Fear of God

Following are five examples from the Word of God which show how Jesus dealt with five entirely different types of fear. The first account is in Matthew 9:2:

And behold, they brought to him a man sick of the palsy, lying on a bed: and Jesus seeing their faith said unto the sick of the palsy; Son, be of good cheer; thy sins be forgiven thee.

17

Examine that verse very closely. Notice the pronoun *their*. In giving this account, the other Gospels reveal that because Jesus was in a very crowded house, and because it was extremely difficult for the friends of the man to get to Him, they let him down through the roof. They actually cut a hole in the roof and let him down into the presence of Jesus so he could receive healing.

The man was sick of the palsy. What is palsy? It is a disease that causes various degrees of shaking and involuntary trembling. Think back to one of the meanings of fear: shaking and trembling!

"But, Marilyn," you may say, "surely you don't think palsy can be caused by fear."

Oh, yes, I do! Look at what Jesus said to this poor man who, shaking and helpless, was in such a bad state when let down through that hole in the roof. The Word says that Jesus saw the faith of the men who had brought the palsied man. He saw *their* faith. This shows how we can have faith for people who are in fear.

Sometimes we say, "If that person just had faith, he wouldn't be like that, he wouldn't be in that condition." I hate to hear that statement come out of the mouth of a Christian! If that person doesn't have faith, **you** need to have faith for him. You have a responsibility.

Notice the term Jesus used when He spoke to the sick man. He didn't just say, "Be of good cheer; thy sins are forgiven thee." He said, *Son, be of good cheer* . . . . That is important! You may say, "Wait a minute, Jesus. This isn't a sin problem; this is a shaking problem. Your saying, *Be of good cheer,* isn't going to help much in this situation."

If you are struggling through a time of depression, and someone comes to you and says, "Oh, snap out of it! Be cheerful! Don't be like that!" you might be able to try that for a few minutes, but you won't keep it up for very long.

But every time Jesus speaks the Word *cheer*, He is dealing with fear. Here in Matthew, cheer means "courage." When Jesus called the man, *Son*, He also said, *Thy sins be forgiven thee*. That man's sins had made him shaky, fearful, and trembling. He was literally scared to death and was shaking because he was a sinner. He was afraid of God.

When Jesus said, *Son*, He was saying, "Relax. You're in the family. God's not mad at you. He loves you!" Jesus stepped into the situation and stood between the man and his fear of God by saying, "Don't worry, Son; your sins are forgiven."

The other men around Jesus at the time got very upset over this saying. The next verses tell us:

And, behold, certain of the scribes said within themselves, This man blasphemeth.

And Jesus knowing their thoughts said, Wherefore think ye evil in your hearts?

For whether is easier, to say, Thy sins be forgiven thee; or to say, Arise, and walk?

20

But that ye may know that the Son of man hath power on earth to forgive sins, (then saith he to the sick of the palsy,) Arise, take up thy bed, and go unto thine house.

Matthew 9:3-6

When this man was set free from his sins (plural), he was set free from fear. When he was set free from fear, he was set free from sickness. See the pattern?

Sin is not always the cause of every sickness. But in this situation, it was. When Jesus said, "I'll stand between your fear and God; I'll take care of the sins," the man was set free. Jesus said, "Be of good courage!" The man was healed from sin, healed from fear, and healed from sickness!

Fear of People

The next example is found in Matthew 9:22:

Jesus turned him about, and when he saw her, he said, Daughter, be of good comfort; thy faith hath made thee whole.

And the woman was made whole from that hour.

The woman mentioned here had an issue of blood for twelve years. When she touched the hem of Jesus' garment, she was healed.

Jesus was on His way to heal the daughter of Jairus, the ruler of the synagogue. The girl was only twelve years old and was about to die. It is interesting that this account is about two women; one was twelve years old and near death, the other had been sick for twelve years. Each received a miracle!

In both instances, faith was involved in order for Jesus to move. The woman who had been ill for twelve years said to herself, *If I may but touch his garment, I shall be whole* (v. 21).

In Mark 11:23 Jesus said, *Whosoever shall say unto this mountain, Be thou removed, and be thou cast into the sea; and shall not doubt in his heart, but shall believe that those things which he saith shall come to pass; he shall have whatsoever he saith.*

The woman **said,** "If I touch His garment, I'll be whole." She would be whole if she touched His garment because she **said** it.

This woman was sneaky about what she was doing. Why? The reason is found in the book of Leviticus. A woman with an issue of blood was not allowed to go into the synagogue or into the temple. She was not allowed to visit anyone's house. In fact, if the ailment didn't stop, her husband was to leave her. She was totally separated from society.

She **was** allowed to go to a small, separate room at the side of the synagogue. It had a small hole in the wall through which she could look into the temple at teaching time. But, basically, she was an outcast from home and society. She couldn't even work for anyone because she was considered unclean.

This explains why this woman was afraid to touch Jesus or even to let Him know what she was going to do. She had a fear: she was afraid of people.

You have to admire her. She did have enough boldness to say to herself, *If I can just touch His garment, I shall be whole,* and then to do it.

In more than one place in the Bible, we read about the hem of a person's garment. Why was the hem so important? At the hem there was sewn a little blue thread and a design with tassels. That blue thread was a sign that the person was obedient to the Word of God and dedicated to following it. When that woman reached through and touched the hem of Jesus' garment, she was touching the Living Word.

Jesus immediately said, *Who touched my clothes?* (Mark 5:30). Jesus and His disciples were probably moving along at a rapid pace through a throng of people. The disciples thought, ''What's wrong with Jesus? We're in a crowd and everybody is touching Him.'' But Jesus said to Himself, *Virtue has gone out of Me.*

(v. 30.) "Virtue" here means "miracle-working power." The Greek word for it is *dunamis.*

In speaking the Word, you release the *dunamis* power of God.

People say, "Oh, if only I had miracle-working power. I want that kind of power." Jesus told His disciples, "If you will tarry in Jerusalem, you'll be endued with power from on high." (Acts 1:8.) That's *dunamis* power! **Spirit-filled people have God's miracle-working power.**

Then why don't we see more Spirit-filled Christians moving in God's miracle-working power? Because it takes the Word to release that power.

There are two kinds of power: *exousia,* or "authority power," and *dunamis,* or "miracle-working power." Jesus used this latter word when He said, *Ye do err, not knowing the scriptures, nor the power (dunamis) of God* (Matt. 22:29).

Jesus was saying, ''The Scriptures give you the authority power. If you don't know the Word, you can't be fully in the flow of God.'' This describes the basic difference between the fundamentalists and the Spirit-filled people. The fundamentalists are heavy on **knowing** the Word. The Pentecostals, the Spirit-filled, the charismatics, are weak on knowing the Word, but heavy on **using** the power of the Word. One group denies the power, but believes the Word. The other group believes in the power, but is lacking in knowledge of the Word. If you are going to be balanced, you must have the Word **and** the power.

After the woman who touched Jesus' garment was healed, she was still afraid. Jesus turned to her and said, *Daughter, be of good comfort; thy faith hath made thee whole.*

If you're a sinner, you don't have to be afraid of God. God loves sinners. Jesus didn't say to the woman, ''You outcast! You unclean thing!'' Instead,

He made her whole—spiritually, mentally, emotionally, and physically. He brought her back into society and made her a somebody. Jesus is always wanting to turn ''nobodies'' into ''somebodies.''

This woman not only feared people and God and her own physical illness, she was probably also afraid because of her poor finances. Another verse tells us that she had spent everything she had for cures, but got no better, only worse. She was probably fearful that, if something didn't happen soon, she would starve. Jesus knew she was in fear. To release her from all her fears, He told her, *Be of good comfort.*

Jesus is saying the same thing to you today to release you from all your fears: ''Be of good cheer!'' You'll see that He wants, *Be of good cheer*, to be a divine order for your life. First, He frees from sin. Secondly, He frees from fear.

Fear of the Unknown

Let's look at another time Jesus used this same phrase. In Matthew 14 we read where Jesus went up into a mountain to pray. He sent His disciples away, telling them to get into a ship and go to the other side of the lake.

And straightway Jesus constrained his disciples to get into a ship, and to go before him unto the other side, while he sent the multitudes away.

And when he had sent the multitudes away, he went up into a mountain apart to pray: and when the evening was come, he was there alone.

But the ship was now in the midst of the sea, tossed with waves: for the wind was contrary.

And in the fourth watch of the night Jesus went unto them, walking on the sea.
                                        Matthew 14:22-25

The Gospel of John gives some further details about this incident.

And when even was now come, his disciples went down unto the sea, and entered into a ship, and went over the sea toward Capernaum . . .

And the sea arose by reason of a great wind that blew.

So when they had rowed about five and twenty or thirty furlongs, they see Jesus walking on the sea, and drawing nigh unto the ship: and they were afraid.

John 6:16-19

The account of this incident in Mark's Gospel says that Jesus actually **saw** the disciples out on the lake. (Mark 6:48.) Think about the timing of **when** Jesus saw them. He was on a mountain praying. It was dark. That little ship was in the middle of the sea having a terrible time. The storm and the wind had surrounded them. Certainly they were not **out** of the will of God because Jesus had told them to cross over.

If the Lord told you to cross the sea during a storm, you might wonder about His reasoning, but you would still obey, wouldn't you? If there is a storm, will He take you across? Yes! He spoke the Word; therefore, we know we're going to get across.

Jesus was on the mountain, watching the disciples toiling at sea. If you have ever been to that area, you know that in the natural you can't see out on the Sea of Galilee at night. It's impossible because it gets so dark there. Actually, even in the daylight you can't see very well. From a mountain you might be able to see that it is windy, or that a storm is raging because the waves are high, but to see a boat would be very difficult, even in daylight. At night, it would be impossible.

Jesus must have "seen" the disciples by the Spirit. He saw them out there in the dark, rowing and rowing with all their might in the raging storm. He followed them with His spiritual eye. Before too long, He went out to the boat by walking on the water. When the disciples saw Him, they were frightened. At first, they thought He was a spirit or a ghost. As He neared the ship, He said, *It is I; be not afraid* (John 6:20).

Sometimes when we begin to do something and an unusual event occurs in the process of our task, we become afraid. We think, *I know Jesus told me to do this, but the storm looks bad. I'm afraid of what's going to happen!* We are afraid of the unknown. But then Jesus comes walking by. He knows we are afraid.

Sometimes people are afraid of Word-based spiritual experiences. A woman once said to me, ''Marilyn, I'm afraid of getting the baptism in the Holy Spirit. When you speak in tongues, does the power come over you so that you can't control yourself anymore? I see people raising their hands and getting very emotional. I don't want to be emotional. Do I have to be so emotional to speak in tongues?''

Because the Spirit of God was unknown and mysterious to her, she was afraid of Him! I think Jesus wanted to say to her, "It is I, the Lord. You don't have to be afraid. I won't make you do anything unseemly." He doesn't make us do anything that does not glorify Him. When a Spirit-filled Christian does something wrong, he is just acting in the flesh. Just because someone else wrecks his brand-new car doesn't keep me from buying a new one!

When the Lord comes to you in a beautiful new way, let Him employ His variety. Don't insist on His behaving the same way every time. It can be different and still be Jesus.

He sees you when you are in those dark times, when it looks like you don't know where you are going. You may be obeying His Word, yet you're rowing and rowing, seemingly getting no place. The winds are contrary and everything is coming against you. But Jesus sees you, and He will meet you there. He won't leave you or forsake you!

*And when the disciples saw him walking
on the sea, they were troubled, saying, It is a
spirit; and they cried out for fear.*

*But straightway Jesus spake unto them,
saying, Be of good cheer; it is I; be
not afraid.*

*And Peter answered him and said, Lord,
if it be thou, bid me come unto thee on
the water.*

Matthew 14:26-28

Impetuous Peter! He wanted to walk
on the water with Jesus, but he knew he
had to have the Word before he could
do it.

Jesus said, *Come* (v. 29).

Peter began walking, then started
looking at the wind and the waves.
Verse 30 says, *But when he saw the wind
boisterous, he was afraid; and beginning to
sink, he cried, saying, Lord, save me.*

Now here is a very unusual
expression: "Beginning to sink." Have
you ever "begun" to sink? When you
dive into the water, do you "begin" to

go into the water and "begin" to sink? No, once you hit the water, you're in!

Peter didn't sink instantly; he started sinking a little bit at a time. Whenever we start looking at circumstances, we start slipping in our faith. We may not go under immediately, but we do "begin to sink" a little.

As soon as Peter began to sink, he cried out to Jesus. Jesus instantly reached out to him, and they both walked back to the ship.

In these accounts of Matthew and John, Jesus said, *It is I; be not afraid.* This is the same as saying, "Be of good cheer! Be of good courage. I am here. I'll take care of you." Whenever we face the mysterious and become afraid, Jesus says, "I'm here. I'll move into the situation. You don't have to be afraid. Be of good cheer. Don't be afraid."

Fear of Failure

Another example of "good cheer" is found in the book of Acts:

And the night following the Lord stood by him, and said, Be of good cheer, Paul: for as thou hast testified of me in Jerusalem, so must thou bear witness also at Rome.

Acts 23:11

Paul was frightened; a mob was out to kill him! Everybody was yelling, screaming, and carrying on! Paul escaped by the skin of his teeth.

Jesus had told him that he was supposed to go to Rome and bring them the Word, but it didn't look like he was going to make it. I think Paul was afraid that his life would be cut short before he got to Rome and that he wouldn't be able to fulfill God's call on his life.

The Lord stood by Paul's side and told him, ''Be of good cheer, Paul!'' That's not like saying, ''Cheer up; put a smile on your face.'' Jesus was saying, ''Be of good courage, Paul, for whereas you have testified of Me in Jerusalem, so must you bear witness of Me also in Rome. I'll get you there!''

When Jesus told Paul to go to Rome, that didn't mean that Paul would have no problems. He had a few—even a shipwreck!

When the storms hit, does that mean that you are out of the will of God? No! It means that you must stand and keep looking at God's Word until the storm passes.

Fear of the World

Another time Jesus said, "Be of good cheer," applies directly to you and me.

These things I have spoken unto you, that in me ye might have peace. In the world ye shall have tribulation: but be of good cheer; I have overcome the world.

John 16:33

Jesus was talking to the disciples. They knew that He was supposed to be King and Messiah, but everything was falling apart around them. Things looked bad!

Jesus had said to them, *Behold, the hour cometh, yea, is now come, that ye shall be scattered, every man to his own, and shall leave me alone: and yet I am not alone, because the Father is with me* (v. 32).

The disciples were probably wondering, "What's going on?" They were afraid of what the world would do to them.

If you are ever afraid of what the world can do to you and your loved ones, remember that Jesus has left His peace for you to dwell in. Because Jesus has overcome the world, you can too! Greater is He Who is in you than he who is in the world! (1 John 4:4.)

Freedom from Fear

Let's review what we have discussed thus far:

To the man who was sick of the palsy, Jesus said, "Son, be of good cheer; your sins are forgiven." In the process of having his sins forgiven, the man was freed from fear.

Even though the man was released from fear, the crowd was filled with fear: *And they were all amazed, and they glorified God, and were filled with fear* (Luke 5:26). What's the difference? **The man who was freed from fear took Jesus into his situation!**

The woman, outcast because of her health, went to Jesus even though she was afraid to approach Him face to face. She had faith. She said, "If I can but touch the hem of His garment, I'll be made whole." She was afraid of being pushed out of the way, and also afraid that Jesus might reject her. She acted in faith and received *dunamis*, the miracle-working power of God, to make her whole.

An important thing to realize concerning fear is that you can quote scriptures against fear all day long, yet remain in fear. I speak Isaiah 54:14 again and again: "Fear and oppression are far from me." Fear is oppression, isn't it? According to the Bible, it is a bondage. But sometimes I don't **feel** like fear is far from me. Why?

Besides confessing the Word, we need to catch a vision of Jesus. We need to see Him between us and the fear. Confess the Word and see Jesus in your situation, standing between you and whatever it is that is trying to attach itself to you.

Jesus spoke to the disciples on the storm-tossed sea and said, "It is I. Don't be afraid." They were afraid until they saw Jesus. When they saw Jesus, their fears left.

The disciples in the upper room were afraid of what the world would do to them. Nobody knew what was going to happen. Jesus told them that He was going to die! But He said, "Don't be afraid. Look at Me. I've overcome the world. I will stand between you and every attack that the world makes against you."

What the world brings along doesn't matter. Get a vision of Jesus standing between you and the problem situation. That's what makes the difference.

Some years ago, when the atheists attacked my television broadcast—a Bible program on educational TV—I could see Jesus standing between the atheists and the TV program. I knew He was there because He said, "I have overcome the world." I didn't have to be afraid of what the world was going to try to do because Jesus has already overcome the world. When the atheistic woman who led the campaign against me went before the TV committee to have my program thrown off the air, they threw her out instead!

The only times recorded in the Bible that Jesus said, "Be of good cheer," are contained in the four examples above. I believe these parallel the four occasions that all mankind faces. When God tells you to do something, but all surrounding evidence makes it look like you can't (as happened with Paul), the Lord will come to help. The people in all these examples saw Jesus.

See Jesus in **your** situation. Confess the Word and have a vision of Jesus standing between you and that which you fear. Remember, the Bible says that without a vision, the people perish. (Prov. 29:18.)

Once I had an invitation to speak at a charismatic conference of Lutherans. The man in charge disliked women teachers. In fact, one time he had told his church, "Don't read any of Marilyn Hickey's books. She is a false prophetess. Don't listen to her on radio and don't watch her telecast because she is wrong. As a woman, she should not be a teacher."

You can imagine my surprise when later a woman from that conference called me to ask, "Would you be a teacher at our conference?"

I thought, *I must be dreaming. That man is head of this conference and here I am being invited to speak there.*

"Do you know whom you are calling?" I asked the lady.

"Isn't your name Marilyn Hickey?"

41

"Yes."

"Can't you do it?"

"My calendar will allow it, but I just can't imagine your inviting me."

But I had such a witness that I was supposed to go that I said, "Yes, I can do it."

When I hung up the phone, I leaned against the wall and said, "Lord, what are You doing?"

Suddenly, I was flooded with fear. I thought, *Is that man inviting me so he can put me on a platform before all those thousands of people and say, "Here is a false prophetess"*? Fear rolled over me.

Then the Holy Spirit said to me, "Marilyn, when I open doors before you, no man can close them. When men open doors before you that are not of Me, I will close them."

When it came time for me to speak at the conference, I had to sit next to that man. Besides that, I was the only woman on the platform. I thought, *He's probably thinking, "I have to sit by you!"* But God said to me, "Stop thinking that way. Hold your peace, and I'll take care of your enemies. Just be quiet."

We are to love our enemies, do good to them, pray for them, bless them. I tried to do all the sweetest things I could think of for that pastor. Eventually, God turned that man's attitude around—so much so that he later invited me to speak four different times in his church!

Types of Fear

We have victory over all the different kinds of fear by speaking faith words and seeing Jesus standing between us and the things we fear.

The Fear of Death

Hebrews 2:15 says, *And deliver them who through fear of death were all their lifetime subject to bondage.*

"Christians shouldn't be afraid of death," you may say.

That's true, but the fact is that many people are afraid of dying. It is not enough to tell them, "Oh, don't be like that!" That is no answer to their fear.

Instead, we need to tell such people, "Jesus will make you free of fear because He has come between you and death. He tasted death for every man. You don't have to be afraid of death because Jesus conquered it. Get a vision of Jesus standing between you and death."

Paul said, *To die is gain* (Phil. 1:21). Why? Because when we die we go to be with Jesus.

The Fear of Evil

This is a terribly evil day in which we live. All kinds of evil things happen: rapes, burglaries, kidnappings, murders, plane crashes, car wrecks. Because we are continually hearing such bad news, we can be hit hard by the fear of evil. But according to Proverbs 1:33, *Whoso hearkeneth unto me shall dwell safely, and shall be quiet from fear of evil.*

The Bible says that in these last days men's hearts will fail them for fear. Did you know that doctors say that eighty percent of all illness is caused by fear? Christians have fears, even those in the faith walk. Though Christians confess the Word, fear can still hang around. Perhaps this occurs because the Christian has no vision of Jesus to go along with his confession.

Jesus is the Word. When you confess scriptures toward your situation, see Jesus in your mind's eye. When the disciples saw Jesus, they weren't afraid any longer. By speaking the Word and seeing Jesus, **your** fears will leave too.

The Fear of War

Psalm 27:3 says, *Though an host should encamp against me, my heart shall not fear: though war should rise against me, in this will I be confident.*

45

We don't need to be afraid of the threat of war—we have a vision of Jesus. We're trusting in Him!

The Fear of Evil Tidings

Whenever I'm on a trip, the Devil really tries to chew on me before I call home. He will say, "What if you call home and find out your daughter has been hurt? or your son has been in an accident? or your church has burned down? or your radio program has been dropped from ten stations? You're going to hear something bad when you call."

Psalm 112:7 is the answer to such fears: *He* (the faithful man) *shall not be afraid of evil tidings: his heart is fixed, trusting in the Lord.*

The Fear of Man

Proverbs 29:25 states, *The fear of man bringeth a snare.*

The following scriptures give the antidote to that fear:

*I, even I, am he that comforteth you:
who art thou, that thou shouldest be afraid
of a man that shall die, and of the son of man
which shall be made as grass;*

*And forgettest the Lord thy maker, that
hath stretched forth the heavens, and laid
the foundations of the earth; and hast feared
continually every day because of the fury of
the oppressor, as if he were ready to destroy?
and where is the fury of the oppressor?*

Isaiah 51:12,13

''Where is the fury of the
oppressor?'' Why are you afraid of
man, anyway? Man will die and pass
away like the grass, but Jesus will be
around to hold you up forever! Never
be afraid of people.

When you see someone who is
afraid, be an encouragement to him.
Instead of saying, ''Too bad. You didn't
make your faith confession every day,
or you wouldn't be afraid,'' go to him
and love him. Stand in faith for him.

Walking in Love

I want to emphasize one more point regarding the man who was sick with the palsy.

When the man's friends brought him to Jesus, he was so afraid that he was shaking. One of the meanings of fear is "to shake." His friends didn't say to him, "Well, if you hadn't been such a sinner, you wouldn't be in this state. You need to repent!"

Faith doesn't work that way! Faith works by love. **We** have no business deciding who has faith and who doesn't. If we know that a certain person is weak in faith, we need to have faith for him.

The Bible says, "Jesus saw **their** faith." Notice what the Scriptures say about the strength of combined faith: *How should one chase a thousand, and two put ten thousand to flight . . . ?* (Deut. 32:30).

When two or more believers put their faith together, they can chase ten thousand! Let's quit criticizing others who have fears as we do, and get busy chasing demons! None of us is as high in faith as he should be. We should see the good in everyone. If we can't see faith in another person, we should pray that he too will be brought into the great place of faith and power which we enjoy.

When we walk in faith, we don't criticize because faith works by love. If we're not moving in love, we're not moving in faith. We can't please God without faith, and faith won't work without love. They go together.

We should quit criticizing, unite our faith, and start confessing the Word for others, loving them. When we do, we will bring them into a place of faith they have never been before.

2
Peter's Triumph Over Fear

Often, fear doesn't leave overnight. One day it may not bother us; the next day it may hit us hard. Fear tends to have a pattern to it.

Let's examine the life of Peter to see where fear took him and how Jesus restored him. By studying the restoration process of Jesus, we can learn how to be free from the cycle of fear.

The first step in overcoming fear is to rebuke it the very moment it comes to us. If we entertain it, it will move in and take over the imagination.

Peter's Profession

Peter said to Jesus, *Thou art the Christ, the Son of the living God* (Matt. 16:16).

That was a marvelous thing for Peter to say. Jesus was really complimented. In return, Jesus said to Peter:

Blessed art thou, Simon Bar-jona: for flesh and blood hath not revealed it unto thee, but my Father which is in heaven.

And I say also unto thee, That thou art Peter, and upon this rock I will build my church; and the gates of hell shall not prevail against it.

Matthew 16:17,18

Peter had made a tremendous statement to Jesus: "You are the Son of God." In response, Jesus said, "You didn't get this from flesh and blood. This is a revelation of the Spirit, and on this statement I will build My Church."

The Church is built, not on Peter, but on his statement, *Thou art the Christ, the Son of the living God.* The Church of

Jesus Christ is not built on a man, but on the fact that Jesus is the Son of God.

Just a few short months after making the greatest statement of the whole New Testament, Peter made the worst one! He denied that he had ever know the man, Jesus of Nazareth! How could one person be so extreme? One time he spoke the best words; the next time, the worst.

Have you ever done anything like that? You confess the Word and have the greatest victories; then five hours later, you blow it. *Oh, God!* you think. *How did I ever do that?* Let's see why that happens so that you will know how to avoid it the next time.

Peter's Denial

Then began he (Peter) *to curse and to swear, saying, I know not the man.*

Matthew 26:74

Peter, the same man who earlier had said, *Thou art the Christ, the Son of the living God,* then proclaimed, ''I don't know the man!'' He cursed and totally denied his Lord.

Why did Peter deny Christ? Why did he get into that position? Peter was afraid! Jesus had been taken prisoner, and Peter was afraid that he too would be thrown into prison.

When the people said to him, "Hey, *you* run around with that Galilean! *You* know who He is!'' Peter's fear rose up, and he began to curse. He didn't want to be connected with Jesus because he was afraid he too would be crucified. Out of fear, Peter denied the Lord.

Most of our wrong statements are made out of fear. When fear comes in, it makes things seem like a mountain. As a result, we make wrong statements.

Most of the time, we don't jump into things. Usually it is a long gradual process that brings us into something good or bad. It's like when we first began to read the Word; we learned precept upon precept, line upon line. (Is. 28:13.)

Building faith is like building character. It is a process. We go from faith to faith, strength to strength, glory to glory. We confess Jesus as our Lord and Savior. That's the first confession, the great confession. As we walk with Him, we begin to learn the Word, confess the Word, and go into higher levels of faith. Faithfulness isn't arrived at overnight.

Mistakes and bad statements are progressive in the same way. They start with one negative thing. If we keep feeding that kind of situation by speaking bad words over it, we begin to go down and down and down! Let's look at Peter's life to find out where he began this process.

After making the tremendous statement, "You are the Christ, the Son of the Living God," Peter got into some trouble. He made a very bad statement. It came right out of his heart, but it was sincerely wrong.

Some people today have lifted up sincerity and said, "If people are sincere, that's all that matters." That's not true. Sincerity is not the answer. We must be sincere about the right thing.

Jesus told His disciples that He was going to die on the cross and be resurrected. When Peter heard this, he began to go wrong:

Then Peter took him, and began to rebuke him, saying, Be it far from thee, Lord: this shall not be unto thee.

Matthew 16:22

Can you imagine anyone having the audacity to tell Jesus what to do? One thing about Peter: he was bold! He made the above statement right after he had confessed Jesus as the Christ. The response Jesus made to Peter shows us that the Church wasn't built upon Peter, but upon his confession of Christ as the Son of God:

He (Jesus) *turned, and said unto Peter, Get thee behind me, Satan: thou art an offence unto me: for thou savourest not the things that be of God, but those that be of men.*

Matthew 16:23

Just six verses earlier Jesus had praised Peter and called him "blessed." Now He is rebuking him and addressing him as "Satan." Why? What did Peter do to go so wrong so quickly?

His first mistake was in trying to say that the cross was wrong. Why did he do that?

You may say, "He did it out of compassion for Jesus!" I don't think so. I think the reason, once again, was fear. Peter was saying, "We've found the Messiah. He's the Son of God. He's going to take us out of Roman rule. He's going to sit on a throne, and we're going to be right beside Him to rule and reign with Him."

Peter failed to see that before the crown came the cross. When Jesus mentioned the cross, Peter thought that did away with the throne. Fear struck Peter and he said, "Oh, no! I won't let You do that!" Peter's first area of fear was fear of the cross.

Our human personalities make us afraid to die to our own desires. We're afraid to say, "Okay, Jesus, I'm willing to surrender all to You." Paul said, *I am crucified with Christ: nevertheless I live; yet not I, but Christ liveth in me* (Gal. 2:20).

We need to be willing to crucify many of our wrong desires. Sometimes we have a fear about what this means, or we want to clutch little things to ourselves. Peter was afraid of the cross. Once that fear crept in, other negative things followed.

Peter began to say things that were not good. (Matt. 26:31-35.) He began to boast, not in the Word, but in himself. The Bible says that we are not to have confidence in the flesh, but rather to have confidence in the Word. If we start boasting in our own strength, having confidence in the flesh, we will get into trouble every time. The following passage reveals Peter's confidence in his own strength:

Then saith Jesus unto them, All ye shall be offended because of me this night: for it is written, I will smite the shepherd, and the sheep of the flock shall be scattered abroad.

But after I am risen again, I will go before you into Galilee.

Peter answered and said unto him, Though all men shall be offended because of thee, yet will I never be offended.

Jesus said unto him, Verily I say unto thee, That this night, before the cock crow, thou shalt deny me thrice.

Peter said unto him, Though I should die with thee, yet will I not deny thee.

Matthew 26:31-35

"I would never do that!" Peter boasted. Christians sometimes talk about others, saying, "Have you heard about so-and-so? He really blew it. I can't understand why he would do something like that. I would never do that!" People who say such things have confidence in the flesh.

We **can** say, "Jesus in me is greater than he who is in the world, and I can do all things through Christ Who strengthens me." Having confidence in the Word will take us through.

Peter had confidence in himself, not in the Word. Fear may take us to the point of saying, "I'm going to be brave!" But we're still putting confidence in the wrong thing. Peter wanted to be brave, but put confidence in himself.

Because of his fear, Peter got into another bad area: a zealousness that was not based on the Word. He couldn't bear to think of Jesus going to the cross. That would have spoiled all his plans.

So when the soldiers came for Jesus, Peter, in his zeal to protect Jesus, took his sword and cut off the ear of the High Priest's servant (Mark 14:47). Peter was trying to keep Jesus from going to the cross because he was afraid of it.

In Mark 14:53,54 we learn of something else that fear did to Peter:

And they led Jesus away to the high priest: and with him were assembled all the chief priests and the elders and the scribes.

And Peter followed him afar off . . . .

Fear will keep us from trusting Jesus; it will cause us to put a distance between us and Him. You may be following Him, but that distance appears because fear doesn't please God. It is faith that pleases God.

Fear is the opposite of faith. When did Peter begin to follow Jesus from a distance? It started the first time he told Jesus, "I'll never let You go to the cross. I'll die before I let You do that!" Peter's words put him in a position of following afar off.

Notice what happened next:

And as Peter was beneath in the palace, there cometh one of the maids of the high priest: and when she saw Peter warming himself, she looked upon him, and said, And thou also wast with Jesus of Nazareth.

But he denied, saying, I know not, neither understand I what thou sayest. And he went out into the porch; and the cock crew.

And a maid saw him again, and began to say to them that stood by, This is one of them.

And he denied it again. And a little after, they that stood by said again to Peter, Surely thou art one of them: for thou art a Galilean, and thy speech agreeth thereto.

But he began to curse and to swear, saying, I know not this man of whom ye speak.

And the second time the cock crew. And Peter called to mind the word that Jesus said unto him, Before the cock crow twice, thou shalt deny me thrice. And when he thought thereon, he wept.

Mark 14:66-72

Peter felt condemned by what he had done because he knew he had acted out of fear. Excusing our false actions by saying, ''I did it because I was afraid,'' doesn't make them right.

Fear led Peter in all these steps. Initially, he was afraid of the cross.

From there his fear grew. He was afraid he was going to have to go to the cross with Jesus, that he might have to die there. His "following afar off" and his denial of Jesus started with fear. Peter should have taken the word of Jesus; instead, Jesus had to tell him, "Get behind Me, Satan. You don't savor the things of God."

The cross is a place of victory, not of defeat. Peter took several steps away from victory, all because of fear.

Peter's Recovery From Fear

Following the steps that brought Peter out of fear will also bring **us** out of fear. But before we examine those steps, I want to point out that we need to start every day with the confession: "Fear and oppression are far from me." (Is. 54:14.) By starting the day this way, we can avoid being attacked by fear.

Fear can be a devilish, hideous thing. The Bible says "fear and oppression" because fear is oppressive;

it is an ugly thing. One of the first statements Adam made was in response to God's question as to why he was hiding. Adam said, "I was afraid." (Gen. 3:10.) He was hiding from God. His fear separated him from God.

God is looking for people who are afraid so that He can bring them out of their fear. That is why there is a plan to set people free from fear.

Let's look at the steps that brought Peter out of fear:

Step One: Hold on to Jesus

And the Lord said, Simon, Simon, behold, Satan hath desired to have you, that he may sift you as wheat:

But I have prayed for thee, that thy faith fail not: and when thou art converted, strengthen thy brethren.

Luke 22:31,32

Jesus called Peter "Simon" on some occasions and "Peter" the rest of the time. Peter is the name Jesus used originally. *Simon* means "hearing."

The first time Jesus called Peter "Simon Bar-jona," He was saying, "Simon, you are a hearing one." When Peter said to Jesus, *Thou art the Christ, the Son of the living God*, Jesus answered, "Simon, flesh and blood didn't reveal this to you. You've been hearing it from the Spirit."

In Luke 22:31,32 Jesus says, "Simon, you've been a hearing one. Satan is going to try to sift you, but I have prayed for you that your faith won't fail. When you are converted, you're going to strengthen the brethren."

Peter responds: *Lord, I am ready to go with thee, both into prison, and to death* (v. 33).

Jesus answers: *I tell thee, Peter, the cock shall not crow this day, before that thou shalt thrice deny that thou knowest me* (v. 34).

Jesus called Peter "Simon" in verse 31 and "Peter" in verse 34. Why? Because He wants Peter to be a hearing one. "Listen to Me, Simon," He is saying. "Satan is going to try to sift you, but don't worry. I have prayed for you that your faith won't fail."

As Jesus said, Peter's faith did not fail, even though his courage did. He did many stupid things, but his faith didn't fail; he went out and wept still believing in Jesus.

Sometimes when we say the wrong things, we feel like we have failed because, after confessing faith, we got into a fear level. Then we say, "I've just blown it. There's no use trying again." **No! This is not true!** Just hang in there with Jesus and say, "I still believe You. I may have blown it. I may have said and done all the wrong things, but somehow I'm still holding on to You." Your courage may fail, but your faith won't.

Jesus said to Peter, "I have prayed for you." Does Jesus pray for *you*? Yes. How do you know? Do you feel it? The Bible tells us Jesus prays for us.

Hebrews 7:25 says that Jesus, seated at the right hand of the Father, ever lives to make intercession for us.

The first step in getting rid of fear is to remember that Jesus is praying for you. When you are afraid, think, *Satan is trying to sift me, but Jesus is praying for me.*

The Bible tells us in Luke 22 that while Peter was denying Jesus, Jesus heard him:

But a certain maid beheld him (Peter) *as he sat by the fire, and earnestly looked upon him, and said, This man was also with him.*

And he denied him, saying, Woman, I know him not.

And after a little while another saw him, and said, Thou art also of them. And Peter said, Man, I am not.

And about the space of one hour after, another confidently affirmed, saying, Of a truth this fellow also was with him: for he is a Galilean.

And Peter said, Man, I know not what thou sayest. And immediately, while he yet spake, the cock crew.

And (then) *the Lord turned, and looked upon Peter . . . .*

Luke 22:56-61

The verb translated here "looked upon" doesn't mean "to look at," it means "to look through." Jesus looked **through** Peter.

What did Jesus think when He looked at Peter? What was He saying in that look? He could have been saying, "Peter, remember how you said that you would die with Me? Remember all those things you were going to do? Peter, I need you the most now; and what are you doing? You are denying Me and cursing. Peter, you really let Me down at the time I needed you the most."

I don't believe His look said that at all. I believe it said, "Peter, don't do this to yourself." Jesus looked **through** Peter.

Step Two: Trust Jesus

The second step in getting rid of fear is to know that Jesus sees us. He sees us right where we are, just as we are. And He loves us as we are, even when we feel that we have let Him and everyone else down. Without condemning us, He looks through us to help us make it.

After the Resurrection, the Bible tells us that Jesus came to His disciples. Remember, the last look that Peter has had from Jesus was while he was denying Him. Now Jesus has risen from the dead. Notice what the angels say in the following passage:

And when the sabbath was past, Mary Magdalene, and Mary the mother of James, and Salome, had bought sweet spices, that they might come and anoint him.

And very early in the morning the first day of the week, they came unto the sepulchre at the rising of the sun.

And they said among themselves, Who shall roll us away the stone from the door of the sepulchre?

And when they looked, they saw that the stone was rolled away: for it was very great.

And entering into the sepulchre, they saw a young man sitting on the right side, clothed in a long white garment; and they were affrighted.

And he saith unto them, Be not affrighted: Ye seek Jesus of Nazareth, which was crucified: he is risen; he is not here: behold the place where they laid him.

But go your way, tell his disciples **and Peter** *. . . .*

Mark 16:1-7

Why didn't the angel just say, "Go tell His disciples"? Because Jesus wanted Peter to have a personal message: "Peter, I'm not mad at you. I know you followed afar off. I know you got in your own zeal and cut off the ear of the priest's servant, and I had to do one of My last miracles because you blew it. I know you cursed. I know you denied Me. But, Peter, I want you to know that it was right for Me to go to the cross. I want you to know that I am risen.''

When you've been in the midst of a real attack of fear, have you ever said, ''God give me a scripture''? Have you ever noticed that Jesus will speak to you personally and give you one? Many times Jesus has impressed into my spirit a specific verse. His sheep know His voice!

One time I was undergoing a very difficult trial. To look at the natural circumstances seemed to me almost unbearable. I said, ''God, I must have something specific from the Word. I know all these scriptures that I claim every day, but I must have something new.''

God gave me a wonderful scripture from Haggai. I had read this book many times without ever seeing this verse as a personal word to me. Whenever the

Devil has tried to hit me with fear about this situation, I quote this verse:

According to the word that I covenanted with you when ye came out of Egypt, so my spirit remaineth among you: fear ye not (Hag. 2:5).

Step Three: Listen to Jesus

The third step in the restoration process is to hear the personal message Jesus has for you.

Jesus not only sent a message to Peter, He also had a personal interview with him after the Resurrection! The Bible tells us in 1 Corinthians 15:5 that *he* (Jesus) *was seen of Cephas* (Peter), *then of the twelve.*

John 20 gives the account of Jesus' appearance before the disciples in the room with all the doors locked. (v. 19.) But before He appeared in that room, Jesus had already appeared to Peter. He wanted to tell Peter that everything was okay.

At times, Jesus wants a personal interview with us. He just wants us to wait in His presence for Him to refresh us. He wants to say, "I'm with you personally."

Have you ever been warmed by His presence? Have you ever awakened in the night to feel fear flooding around you, then to feel the presence of Jesus come in and have all the fear to leave?

Remember, Jesus said, *I will never leave thee nor forsake thee* (Heb. 13:5). People have had personal interviews with God many times.

Wait in God's presence. He has a personal time for **you,** too!

Some of us might say, "Jesus could have been angry with Peter; maybe that's the reason He wanted to meet with him in private." But Jesus isn't angry with people who are afraid. He is praying for them and trying to bring them out of their fear.

This is how we should be, too. We shouldn't become upset with people who are afraid. We ought not say, "They're just not in faith." If we are in faith, we need to bring those people out of fear and into faith by lifting them up and giving them the Word.

Peter's Restoration

Jesus deals with Peter because Peter has been fearful and unbelieving. (John 21:15-22.) Someone might say, "Jesus still loves Peter." Yes, but Jesus had to deal with Peter right where he was, right where the stem of the fear was. Peter had to face his fear in order to be set free. Sympathy will never set us free from fear, but God's Word will!

After these things Jesus shewed himself again to the disciples at the sea of Tiberias; and on this wise shewed he himself.

There were together Simon Peter, and Thomas called Didymus, and Nathanael of Cana in Galilee, and the sons of Zebedee, and two other of his disciples.

Simon Peter saith unto them, I go a fishing.

John 21:1-3

In the Greek, Peter was actually saying, "I'm going back to the fishing trade." This wasn't just a little vacation trip Peter had planned. He meant to return to his former occupation.

You might say, "Marilyn, do you mean that after Peter has had a personal interview with Jesus, he's going back to the fishing business?"

Yes he is, because there's still something about the cross that's bothering him. Whenever a leader turns back, he always takes some people with him. Peter invited some of the key disciples to come with him, and they went.

After fishing all night from a ship, they caught nothing. Jesus uses this experience also to deal with Peter:

When the morning was now come, Jesus stood on the shore: but the disciples knew not that it was Jesus. Then Jesus saith unto them, Children . . . .

John 21:4,5

The Greek word *paidion*, used here to address the disciples, is not the usual word for children in general. It refers to children who are under training. When Jesus used it, it was as though He were saying, "Students, I'm about to teach you something today."

. . . Children, have ye any meat? They answered him, No.

And he said unto them, Cast the net on the right side of the ship, and ye shall find.
John 21:5,6

You may wonder why the disciples threw the net over, not knowing that it was Jesus telling them to do so.

The water is so clear in the Sea of Galilee that it is easy to see where the great schools of fish are located because they form dark shadows under the water. Sometimes men would stand on the hillside where they could see the dark shadows in the water, then yell at the fishermen in their boats and direct them to the schools of fish. If someone were to yell out from the shore, "Cast on the right side,'' the fishermen would think, *There's a school of fish over there.*

According to the Bible, the disciples did what Jesus said. They cast their net on the other side, and *they were not able to draw it for the multitude of fishes* (v. 6).

There were seven strong men in the boat—Simon, Thomas, Nathanael, the two sons of Zebedee, and two other disciples—and the catch was so big that they couldn't handle it.

Therefore that disciple whom Jesus loved saith unto Peter, It is the Lord. Now when Simon Peter heard that it was the Lord, he girt his fisher's coat unto him (for he was naked,) and did cast himself into the sea (v. 7).

That's typical of Peter, isn't it? Always doing something impulsive. He swam toward shore, while the other disciples came in a little boat taken from the larger fishing boat. They had a difficult time dragging in that net with the fish. There were only six of them left because Peter had jumped into the water!

As soon then as they were come to land, they saw a fire of coals there, and fish laid thereon, and bread.

Jesus saith unto them, Bring of the fish which ye have now caught.

Simon Peter went up, and drew the net to land full of great fishes, an hundred and fifty and three . . . .

John 21:9-11

How did Peter do that when six men couldn't do it before? He had seen Jesus!

When we begin to get a vision of Jesus, the Bible says we can do all things through Christ Who strengthens us. (Phil. 4:13.) Peter began to receive the strength of Christ as soon as he saw Him, even though he had been in error again. He was running from his call, but he still pulled all those fish to the shore by himself. Once Peter pulls in the fish, Jesus deals with him.

Notice that Jesus had built a fire. Where was it that Peter had denied

Jesus? By a fire! When Peter saw that fire, he must have thought, *Oh, yes. I remember the last fire I was by with You, Jesus. I cursed then and denied You.*

Jesus wanted to show Peter something else by having that fire there: **We don't have to camp by the enemy's fire.** The Bible says that Jesus can set our hearts on fire. The two men who walked with Jesus on the road to Emmaus said later, *Did not our heart burn within us, while he talked with us by the way, and while he opened to us the scriptures?* (Luke 24:32).

Just be sure to get the right fire—the Holy Spirit, not the enemy's fire. The Devil will burn you out; Jesus will give you a "holy heartburn." Jesus is building a fire which doesn't hurt. It gives us boldness.

Instead of calling Peter into court and accusing him, saying, "Peter, you did this and this and this," Jesus had prepared breakfast for him. (Notice that Jesus met Peter's physical needs first.

Usually, we think the physical needs come last, but we see here that Jesus is very concerned about our physical needs.)

After Jesus has met Peter's needs, He says to him, *Simon, son of Jonas . . .* (Remember, when Jesus calls Peter "Simon," He wants him to hear. He means, "Are you listening?") . . . *lovest thou me more than these?* (John 21:15).

In other words, Jesus was asking him, "Simon Peter, do you love Me more than you do this fishing trade?"

"Yes, Lord, You know I love You," Peter answers.

The word for love which Jesus uses here is *agape:* "Do you love Me with a love that gives and expects nothing back?"

When Peter answers, however, he uses a different word for love, *phileo:* "Lord, I said I would die for You. I said I wouldn't deny You, but I blew it! I don't love You with the kind of love that gives and expects nothing back."

Peter is so honest. He says, "I just love You with reciprocal love. You love me and I love You back. I love You like a friend."

Then Jesus says, *Feed my lambs* (v. 15). The word *feed* means "to give them the best of nourishment." Notice that Jesus says "lambs," the little ones.

Again, Jesus says, *Simon, son of Jonas, lovest thou me?* (v. 16). "Do you love Me with *agape* love, a love that would die for Me?"

"Lord, You know how I love You," says Peter. "I love You with *phileo* love. Lord, You know that because You know me!"

Feed my sheep (v. 16). A different word for *feed* is used here. It means "discipline and training." Jesus is saying, "Train My sheep." He also says "sheep," not "lambs," because you *feed* lambs, but you *train* sheep. "Feed My sheep—discipline them, educate them, train them."

81

Jesus says to Peter the third time, *Simon, son of Jonas, lovest thou me?* (v. 17). But this time He uses the word *phileo:* "Do you even love Me with that kind of reciprocal love?"

Peter is grieved because Jesus asks him this question three times. He says to Jesus, "Do You doubt that I love You even with that kind of love? Lord, You know everything. You know that I do love You."

Again, Jesus says to Peter, *Feed my sheep* (v. 17). Here Jesus uses the word for feed which has the first meaning. He is saying, "Give My sheep the best nourishment you can give! Older sheep need to be fed as well as little lambs, and older sheep need to be trained."

How many times does Peter deny Jesus? Three.

How many times does Jesus ask Peter if he loves Him? Three.

Peter says, "I love You. I love You. I love You. I may not love You with the love I should, but I love You."

At one time, I was disappointed in a family who was attending our church. They had many problems, and my husband and I had spent much time counseling them, praying with them, and working with their children. But they turned against us, said some malicious things about the ministry, and denounced the baptism in the Holy Spirit.

While doing some radio taping on a Saturday afternoon, I was teaching from John, chapter 21. In my heart I felt wounded by this family, but when I read, "Simon, do you love Me? Feed My sheep," and taught that twice Jesus had used *agape* love, the Lord spoke to me. He said, "Marilyn, I have called you to feed sheep. I have called you to feed them the Word. But you have to love them with *agape* love, which means you must love them expecting nothing in return. You are expecting something back!"

That was a blow! I expected that family to be nice to me because I had been feeding them.

God said, "If you are going to be a sheep-feeder, you must have the heart and the love that I have."

"Lord," I said, "I'll love them, even if they kick me in the teeth." And they did! But I continued to love them!

If you are going to feed sheep, don't think that all the sheep will think you are great. They won't. Don't expect every sheep to come up and say, "What a dynamite lesson!" Just feed them and love them; feed them and love them. It takes *agape* love to be a sheep-feeder.

Peter's Deliverance

Finally, Jesus deals with the point at which Peter's fear began:

Verily, verily, I say unto thee, When thou wast young, thou girdest thyself, and walkedst whither thou wouldest: but when thou shalt be old, thou shalt stretch forth thy hands, and another shall gird thee, and carry thee whither thou wouldest not.

This spake he, signifying by what death he should glorify God. And when he had

spoken this, he saith unto him, Follow me.
John 21:18,19

What kind of death is Jesus talking about for Peter? Death on the cross! According to history, this is the way Peter died. This type of death is pictured in the above passage, and Peter is the one who is frightened of crosses! Jesus is saying, ''Peter, don't be afraid of the cross. You're going to die on one, too.''

History records that when preparations were being made to crucify Peter, he said, ''No, I'm not worthy to die like my Lord.'' So, at his own request, he was crucified upside down. Jesus took the fear out of Peter.

If someone said to me, ''Marilyn, you're going to die on a cross,'' I would think, *Well, I'm never going to a foreign country to pass out tracts!* Wouldn't you?

But Jesus so delivers us from fear that we are willing to go to the cross; it doesn't matter. We will be victorious anyway because we always triumph in Christ. (2 Cor. 2:14.)

Jesus is saying, ''Peter, that cross you are so afraid of, that you don't want Me to go to . . . look, it's My resurrection. And, Peter, you're going to go to it, too; but you won't be worried about it or afraid. I'm taking you right to the cross—and out of it.''

What a powerful deliverance from fear!

Peter's Commission

Then Peter, turning about, seeth the disciple whom Jesus loved following; which also leaned on his breast at supper, and said, Lord, which is he that betrayeth thee?

Peter seeing him saith to Jesus, Lord, and what shall this man do?

John 21:20,21

After reading this, we want to say, ''Oh, Peter, don't you have enough to handle without wondering about everyone else?''

Jesus saith unto him, If I will that he tarry till I come, what is that to thee? follow thou me.

John 21:22

In other words, Jesus was saying, "Peter, just keep your eyes on Me. I'm going to take you through."

Not only has Jesus restored Peter from fear, forgiven him for his mistakes, gone to him and dealt with him directly; He has brought him back into the ministry, which is where Peter should have been all along.

Jesus is saying, "Get out of fish, and get into sheep." At one time Jesus had said to Peter, "You'll fish for men." (Matt. 4:19.) But now He says, "You'll feed My sheep." (John 21:16,17.)

Peter's Reformation

Did Peter change? He surely did! If you think Peter is still afraid, you are wrong. Read Acts, chapter 2:

But Peter, standing up with the eleven, lifted up his voice, and said unto them, Ye men of Judea, and all ye that dwell at Jerusalem . . . (v. 14).

Peter then follows this introduction with a powerful sermon. This is the day of Pentecost—three thousand souls are converted this day! Peter could have been killed for his sermon. Is this the Peter of fear? No! This is the Peter who has been restored from fear, the Peter who says, "It doesn't matter; I can go to the cross. I'm not afraid: Jesus is with me; He is in me." This is the Peter who could say with Paul, "I can do all things through Christ Who strengthens me."

Personality reactions are interesting—they reveal what a person is really like. Once Paul corrected Peter heavily by saying, "Peter, you wouldn't eat with the Gentile brethren; you got involved with dissimulation. You tried to act holier than the Gentile believers. You did wrong!" (Gal. 2:14.)

But nowhere in either of Peter's epistles do we read that Peter was angry with Paul. Peter's old man was dead. Because he was already living in the cross, he was victorious. Even after being corrected by him, Peter referred to Paul as *our beloved brother Paul* (2 Pet. 3:15).

In so many words, Peter was saying, "He was right; I was wrong; and I'm willing to admit it. I've been to the cross, and I'm dead anyway."

Our Confidence

Dead men don't scream. Dead flesh doesn't scream. If our flesh is screaming, we haven't reckoned it dead at the cross. We are afraid of the cross, but the cross is the place of our victory! All our fears died 2000 years ago on the cross.

What Jesus wants to say to us today is: "Are you a Simon? Are you a hearing one? Are you hearing what I'm saying to you?"

You may say, "Oh, I'm zealous!" That's great. Be zealous, but be sure you are zealous in the Word.

Fear itself is a phobia. It's so ugly because it seems to possess a person and not let him go. That's why Jesus was always saying, "Don't be afraid.

Fear not.'' When fear comes, we need to begin immediately to dismiss it.

Isaiah 26:3 says, *Thou wilt keep him in perfect peace, whose mind is stayed on thee: because he trusteth in thee.* Jesus will keep us in peace; we don't have to worry.

Romans 8:15 says that we have not received the spirit of bondage. Fear is a bondage. We saw how Peter was bound by fear. Rather we have received the Spirit of adoption whereby we can say, ''Father, help me.'' And He does help!

Jesus didn't give us fear. Second Timothy 1:7 says, *For God hath not given us the spirit of fear; but of power, and of love, and of a sound mind.* Psalm 34:4 says, *I sought the Lord, and he heard me, and delivered me from all my fears.*

We don't have to be afraid when we hear the newscasters predict wars. Psalm 27:3 says, *Though an host should encamp against me, my heart shall not fear: though war should arise against me, in this will I be confident.*

People say that the whole economy of America is going down the drain. But we don't need to worry about this because Proverbs 1:33 says, *But whoso hearkeneth unto me shall dwell safely, and shall be quiet from fear of evil.*

Fear causes heart attacks! In Luke 21:26, Jesus speaks of *men's hearts failing them for fear, and for looking after those things which are coming on the earth: for the powers of heaven shall be shaken.*

If any of us are afraid of the future, we shouldn't be—there is nothing to be afraid of. Psalm 112:7 says of the faithful man, *He shall not be afraid of evil tidings: his heart is fixed, trusting in the Lord.* When we hear bad tidings, we should say immediately, "My heart is fixed. I'm trusting in the Lord. My heart is fixed on Him."

It's not good to be around people who are afraid because fear is contagious. Isaiah 8:12 says, *Neither fear ye their fear, nor be afraid.* When we do have to be around people who are fearful, we need to remember 1 Peter 3:14 which says, *And be not afraid of their terror, neither be troubled.*

Proverbs 28:1 tells us, *The wicked flee when no man pursueth: but the righteous are bold as a lion.* Peter ran around like a chicken with its head cut off. He followed afar off and ran away when no one was even after him! The people were after Jesus, not Peter. That's an example of what fear does. But faith, the opposite of fear, makes us bold.

Be bold! When something bad happens, just get bolder in Jesus. Say, "Devil, if you think I'm going under, I'm not—I'm going over! I'm going to be bolder than I've ever been before!"

Let your flesh and fears die at the cross. Experience a resurrection of life, living with Jesus.

When Jesus took Peter to the cross and delivered him, Peter was never afraid again. Let Jesus take **you** to the cross to deliver **you** from all your fears!

3

You Are a Giant in Jesus

''I was afraid.'' This was one of the first statements Adam made. The following scripture shows us the root of all fear:

And there we saw the giants, the sons of Anak, which come of the giants: and we were in our own sight as grasshoppers, and so we were in their sight.

Numbers 13:33

This statement was made by the ten spies of Israel when they had come back from seeing the Promised Land. Twelve returned, but ten of them gave an evil report.

An evil report is having the wrong self-image, the wrong faith image. It is always an evil report when we see ourselves as grasshoppers, as something people can walk on. When we allow such a false image into our minds and hearts, fear enters in.

The ten said, "When we saw ourselves as grasshoppers, the giants saw us that way, too!"

The "Grasshopper Complex"

When we see ourselves as nothing, as grasshoppers, other people look on us in the same way. One of the most dangerous things we Christians can do is to see ourselves in the natural realm—to see all of our defeats, failures, and flops, instead of seeing Jesus in us.

"Grasshopper complexes" are very dangerous.

Grasshoppers were major enemies of Israel. Hoards of them consumed Israel's crops. The words *grasshopper* and *locust* are used interchangeably in the Scriptures because they refer to the same insect.

94

Grasshoppers were supposed to be food for the Israelites, according to Leviticus 11:22. How did they cook them? They roasted them lightly, then dried them in the sun. Supposedly when prepared this way, they taste like shrimp. We could say that the grasshopper is the poor man's shrimp.

When the spies came back, they were saying, ''We and our children (they spoke the same negative image for their offspring) will be meat for the giants! They will eat us because people eat grasshoppers.''

In the Book of Judges we read about Gideon, who also had a poor self-image. When an angel appeared to him and said, *The Lord is with thee, mighty man of valour* (Judges 6:12), Gideon said, ''Who, me? Do you know who I am? I'm the poorest in my family, and my family is the poorest in Manasseh. I'm nothing but a flop. I've always been defeated; I've always failed.''

But God took Gideon step by step out of that poor self-image. He led him out to win great victories, shouting, *The sword of the Lord, and of Gideon* (Judges 7:18).

He taught Gideon to call himself a victor in battle. God changed Gideon's concept and perception of himself. He told him, ''Don't see yourself as a grasshopper, Gideon. See the enemy as the grasshopper. You step on grasshoppers.''

God said that it was not Gideon who was the grasshopper, but rather it was Israel's enemy, the Midianites who were the insects:

For they came up with their cattle and their tents, and they came as grasshoppers for multitude; for both they and their camels were without number: and they entered into the land to destroy it.

Judges 6:5

Grasshoppers are mentioned again in the Book of Job:

Canst thou make him afraid as a grasshopper? the glory of his nostrils is terrible.

Job 39:20

This is saying, "Can you make the enemy afraid like a little grasshopper would be?"

Do you see yourself as a grasshopper before the giants of your life? Do you think, *I am like a grasshopper. A giant could just come and walk on me*?

A grasshopper is afraid because everything is bigger than he is. The Israelites saw not only the giants as larger than they were, they saw everything as larger than they. To people in fear, everything in their life is a giant.

Also when they shall be afraid of that which is high, and fears shall be in the way, and the almond tree shall flourish, and the grasshopper shall be a burden, and desire shall fail: because man goeth to his long home, and the mourners go about the streets.

Ecclesiastes 12:5

This indicates that man will even be afraid of the lowly grasshopper. *The grasshopper shall be a burden.* Remember, in the Bible the word *grasshopper* is always used in connection with fear:

> *It is he that sitteth upon the circle of the earth, and the inhabitants thereof are as grasshoppers; that stretcheth out the heavens as a curtain, and spreadeth them out as a tent to dwell in.*
>
> *Isaiah 40:22*

In this description we see that God is sitting on the circle, or sphere, of the earth. (In Columbus' day, men believed the world was flat; but here in the Book of Job, God talks about the earth being round.)

God looks down from heaven and says, "Those people look as small as grasshoppers. I can send Gideon out and he will walk all over them." God always looked at the enemies of mankind as grasshoppers. Remember that God told the Israelites who came back from the Promised Land, "The giants are the ones who are the grasshoppers; you are the giants!"

God's View of You

Greater is he that is in you, than he that is in the world (1 John 4:4).

God working with and within us can overcome anything. But fear makes us think of ourselves as grasshoppers, giving us a bad self-image. Even psychiatrists and psychologists say that this is the greatest problem anyone can have. When Jesus comes into our heart, He gives us a whole new self-image.

Exodus, chapter 10, tells us that the eighth plague to come upon the Egyptians was locusts, or grasshoppers, which ate up all of the crops. But God sent a wind and blew them away. God knows how to take away all the ''grasshopper'' fears that we could ever have. He has done away with grasshoppers, so we don't have to worry about them.

Let's consider the structure of the grasshopper. He has six legs, four of which he uses to walk, and the two larger back legs are for jumping. This gives him leverage to hop, or jump in the air, in a forward motion.

The female grasshopper bores a small hole in the earth and plants her eggs, usually in the spring—April or May. The incubation time is about six weeks, after which out comes a little grasshopper. At this stage of development, he is still in the pupae stage and not very complete. His wings are still in a case so he can't fly, and his back legs are not sufficiently developed to give him the spring he needs to jump. But even if he can't move about very effectively, he has a voracious appetite. This is when he eats the most, and he eats everything in sight!

I thought about this, and about how the Devil comes and plants a little egg of fear in us. Maybe it's planted when we are children. A parent may say, ''You never do anything right! You're always stumbling and clumsy. You're the clumsiest child I've ever seen!'' Right then that little egg of fear is planted in the spirit of that small child.

As he grows up, he thinks, *I'll always be clumsy!* The little egg has begun to incubate in his mind. He keeps hearing negative statements, and perhaps even his friends at school reinforce it. "You clumsy ox!" When he drops a pencil, his teacher says, "Stupid! What's wrong with you? You're always dropping things!"

What happens? By the time he is a young man of seventeen or eighteen, he has developed a clear image of himself as clumsy and stupid. Fear comes right out in the open and chews on him. Because grasshoppers have little teeth, that's exactly how they eat: by chewing and chewing and chewing.

Fear starts like that, too. Fear is planted in the subconscious. Like an egg it lays there and grows and develops. It chews on the personality until the person comes to see himself as a grasshopper.

The Bible says that God blew away grasshoppers with a wind. He said, "I see the enemy as your grasshoppers; I don't see you as a grasshopper." I want to encourage you about fears that may have been planted in you.

God tells us in Joel 2:25, *I will restore to you the years that the locust hath eaten.* When we come to the Father and see who we are, those years of fear drop away. We suddenly realize that we have been made the righteousness of God in Christ Jesus. (2 Cor. 5:21.) We begin to think, *I can do all things through Christ Who strengthens me.* (Phil. 4:13.)

Our self-image changes. Now we can say, "I am more than a conqueror through Him Who loved me." (Rom. 8:37.) "I can overcome every fiery dart the enemy sends against me because I have faith in the Son." (Eph. 6:16.)

We begin to see who we are in Christ. And what happens to those years that the locust destroyed, when the Devil convinced us we were never going to be worthwhile? They are suddenly blown away in the light of God's Word! That's why it is so important for Christians to see who they are in Christ.

There are people who say, "Yes, but the poor Israelites didn't get to go in and take the Promised Land for forty years."

They weren't allowed to do so because all those who came back from that Promised Land with an image of themselves as grasshoppers had to die like grasshoppers out in the wilderness. They had that image of themselves, and they stayed in that image. They didn't take the Word image—God's viewpoint —and because of it, they perished in the desert.

You might say, "If only they hadn't looked at the giants." No, it wasn't the giants who kept them out of the Promised Land; it was their grasshopper complex.

Sometimes we look around and say, "Oh, if I could just do this or that, but I don't have the talent or the ability." Or, "If I just weren't married to this person,

I could really be spiritual." Or, "If I didn't have to go to this church, I would probably be a great evangelist." Or, "If I just had a good job or a better education, then I could really do something for God."

It's not your mate, or the church you attend, or your job, or education, or lack of education that is keeping you from what God has for you. It's fear! It was the grasshoppers that kept the children of Israel out of the Promised Land, not the giants.

As long as we see ourselves as grasshoppers, that attitude will keep us from the promises of God. When you begin to take God's viewpoint of yourself as outlined in His Word, then you will overcome that grasshopper image.

Do you know how you will see yourself? You will say, "I'm a giant."

Do you remember what John the Baptist did with grasshoppers and locusts? He ate them! What does God want you to do with your fears? Eat them. Eat your fears. You do that by quoting the Word of God to them.

In righteousness shalt thou be established: thou shalt be far from oppression; for thou shalt not fear: and from terror; for it shall not come near thee.

Isaiah 54:14

Jesus repeatedly said, "Fear not! Fear not!" Begin to eat up your fears with the Word.

Four Steps to Freedom from Fear

There once was a man who was never dominated by fear. We are going to see how he started in that position, and how he stayed there, free of fear. We will see the Word of God coming forth in his life, making him a conqueror, taking him into places of tremendous responsibility and power:

In the third year of the reign of Jehoiakim king of Judah came Nebuchadnezzar king of Babylon unto Jerusalem, and beseiged it.

And the Lord gave Jehoiakim king of Judah into his hand, with part of the vessels

105

of the house of God: which he carried into the land of Shinar to the house of his god; and he brought the vessels into the treasure house of his god.

And the king spoke unto Ashpenaz the master of his eunuchs, that he should bring certain of the children of Israel, and of the king's seed, and of the princes;

Children (youths) in whom was no blemish, but well favoured, and skilful in all wisdom, and cunning in knowledge, and understanding science, and such as had ability in them to stand in the king's palace, and whom they might teach the learning and the tongue of the Chaldeans.

Daniel 1:1-4

The physical description of these young men indicates that they were extremely good looking and physically fit. They conducted themselves well.

Nebuchadnezzar said that these were the kinds of people he wanted to train to be his counselors. Then he appointed for them certain types of food and drink so they could be well nourished. He wanted to make them even more fit than they already were. At the end of three years they would stand before the king for his approval. Notice that these included the children of Judah, young Israelites.

At this time the king gave these young men of Judah new names:

Now among these were of the children of Judah, Daniel, Hananiah, Mishael, and Azariah:

Unto whom the prince of the eunuchs gave names: for he gave unto Daniel the name of Belteshazzar; and to Hananiah, of Shadrach; and to Mishael, of Meshach; and to Azariah, of Abednego.

Daniel 1:6,7

Why did the king's servant change Daniel's name? Because he wanted to change Daniel's image of himself. Daniel means "God judges," or "one whom God judges." It was a spiritual name given by the family. When you follow through the names of people in the Bible, you will find that families always named their children what they wanted them to become. Daniel would make judgments as God would judge.

The Chaldeans said, "We don't want him to have that image of himself. His God is big in him. His God can judge truth, and Daniel is a judge on the earth." So Nebuchadnezzar decided, "Let's call him Belteshazzar," meaning "one whom Bel judges," or "one in whom Bel lives." Bel was the major idol of Nebuchadnezzar.

They said, "Daniel, we'll change your name because you have the wrong image of yourself. We'll give you a new name and a new image. You'll think that you belong to the idol Bel."

But Nebuchadnezzar was not successful. Changing Daniel's name did not change his self-image.

The world wants to change your image of yourself. When you say, "I am more than a conqueror; I can do all things through Christ Who strengthens me; I can quench all the fiery darts of the enemy with the Word of God," the world says, "Oh, yeah?" They begin to tempt you and change you so you won't be like God and won't see yourself as God sees you. They want you to see yourself the way the Devil sees you. He wants you to have a poor self-image, and he does his best to prove to you that this image is the real you.

The Chaldeans changed Daniel's name, but they were unable to change his self-image. They also changed the names of Daniel's friends. They were renamed Shadrach, Meshach, and Abednego—names which had different spiritual meanings than their Hebrew names.

Step One: Purpose

There are four things, four "P's," that will keep you with the image of a giant instead of a grasshopper. Here is the first one:

*But Daniel **purposed** in his heart that he would not defile himself with the portion of the king's meat . . . .*
Daniel 1:8

Daniel **purposed** in his heart that he was not going to change. He would not be like the others! *My name is Daniel*, he thought. *Whether they call me stupid, clumsy, dumb, a dope, or a jerk, I am still Daniel. That's who I am.* He purposed this before he received his name change.

You need to purpose in your heart right now who **you** are. Then when you go out to face the world, and they say all those negative things about you, it will not affect you because you will have already purposed who and what you are.

What is **your** purpose? Daniel purposed that he would not defile himself with the king's meat.

. . . nor with the wine which he drank: therefore he requested of the prince of the eunuchs that he might not defile himself.
Daniel 1:8

Daniel said to himself, *I am not getting into drunkenness. I have purposed in my heart that I am not going to eat the kind of food that is offered to idols. You may call me Belteshazzar, but I am Daniel, and Daniel means "God judges." God judges that this is wrong for me. I've made a purpose that I am a giant and not a grasshopper.*

Don't switch images, no matter what the world calls you. You know who you are. You belong to God. He lives in you.

Now God had brought Daniel into favour and tender love with the prince of the eunuchs.

Daniel 1:9

When Daniel purposed in his heart, God gave him favor with the prince of eunuchs. God wants to give us favor with non-Christians, with the world. When we purpose in our hearts to be giants and not grasshoppers, the world likes that attitude. The world has always liked giants, but they have never

111

liked grasshoppers. They get rid of grasshoppers. Don't be a grasshopper—be a giant! It will bring you favor.

Do you like to be around grass-hopper Christians? Do you like to associate with fearful, negative, faithless Christians? **No!** When you have been with them, you want to go home, take a bath, and wash your mind out because of all the unbelief that was spoken to you.

But then the Bible tells us that Daniel's stand caused a problem for the prince of the eunuchs. He was afraid that if he allowed these four men not to eat the king's prescribed food and drink, he would be punished or even killed if they looked worse than the others. So Daniel told him:

Prove (test) *thy servants, I beseech thee, ten days; and let them give us pulse* (vegetables) *to eat, and water to drink.*

Then let our countenances be looked upon before thee.

Daniel 1:12,13

The eunuch agreed. For ten days the four ate what they knew to be their correct diet.

And at the end of ten days their countenances appeared fairer and fatter in flesh than all the children which did eat the portion of the king's meat.

Daniel 1:15

Christians should look better than anyone else because we have been eating the Word and drinking the Water of Life. That's the most nourishing food and drink you can have!

I encourage you to systematically read through the Bible so that you have a daily Bible-reading pattern. You cannot chew on a scripture twice a week and come out looking better than the world. It is that daily eating and drinking and praying in the Spirit that does the job.

Before Daniel ever faced the trial, he purposed in his heart, ''I am not going to be defiled.'' Before you go any place, purpose in your heart, ''I am the giant, not the grasshopper, in this place. I will not defile myself with the world.'' Purpose in your heart and you will look better than anyone else.

As for these four children (young men), *God gave them knowledge and skill in all learning and wisdom: and Daniel had understanding in all visions and dreams.*

Daniel 1:17

When you purpose in your heart to be the giant of the situation, to let the Word of God be the judge of it, to let the Word live big in you before everything else, God will step in. When you let the Word be the biggest thing in your life, then God begins to give you the other things as well.

At the end of the three years of training, these four were wiser than anyone else. Why? Because the Word says, *Seek ye first the kingdom of God, and his righteousness; and all these* (other) *things shall be added unto you* (Matt. 6:33).

That's exactly what happened. Daniel and his friends looked better and performed better than anyone else.

Aren't Christians supposed to look and perform better than non-Christians? You should look the best of anyone on your job. You should be the best student in school. You should be the best in every area of your life—the best dressed, the best looking, the most intelligent of any group you are a part of. That's what God's Word says.

But in order for that to happen, you have to purpose in your heart that you are not going to be defiled, that you are going to put God first. You must purpose to let His Word be the judge, that you are going to be addicted to the Word. Then you will go into any situation as a giant and not a grasshopper.

Step Two: Prayer

The second thing Daniel did was **pray.** The Bible tells us that, in the second year of his reign, Nebuchadnezzar had a dream. Though the dream was very real to him, he could not remember what it was.

Eastern monarchs of that day put much stock in dreams, and this was a spiritual dream, a message from God to Nebuchadnezzar. (Today we would call it a revelation.)

Nebuchadnezzar called in all of his wise men and said to them, ''I want you to tell me what I dreamed, then give me its interpretation. If you don't do this, I will kill all of you.'' (Dan. 2:1-9.)

The wise men answered the king:

There is not a man upon the earth that can shew the king's matter: therefore there is no king, lord, nor ruler, that asked such things at any magician, or astrologer, or Chaldean.

And it is a rare thing that the king requireth, and there is none other that can shew it before the king, except the gods, whose dwelling is not with flesh.

Daniel 2:10,11

They said, ''We can't tell you this dream! The gods would have to tell us. You, King, tell us what you dreamed and we will tell you the interpretation. Anyone could make up an interpretation—but to tell you the dream, too? We can't do that!"

So the king said, "I've supported you wise men long enough. For years I have supported you out of my coffers. Now by your own admission you cannot do what I ask." So he issued a decree that all the wise men in the land were to be killed, including Daniel and his friends.

Then Daniel went in, and desired of the king that he would give him time, and that he would shew the king the interpretation.

Then Daniel went to his house, and made the thing known to Hananiah, Mishael, and Azariah, his companions:

That they would desire the mercies of the God of heaven concerning this secret; that Daniel and his fellows should not perish with the rest of the wise men of Babylon.

Daniel 2:16-18

First Daniel purposed, then he prayed. Daniel did not pray just when he got into trouble. He had a pattern of praying:

He kneeled upon his knees three times a day, and prayed, and gave thanks before his God.

Daniel 6:10

It is very important to purpose in your heart right now to be a person who is disciplined in reading the Word daily, and then to have a set time for prayer. I do not believe in now-and-again Bible reading or in hit-or-miss prayer times. If you live like that, you will never be a giant, but always a grasshopper Christian.

It is true that you can pray anytime, but notice that Daniel prayed three times a day. He had a definite prayer pattern.

I believe that everyone should pray early in the morning. In Proverbs 8:17 God tells us, *Those that seek me early shall find me.* I think there is great wisdom here.

In the morning your mind is freshest. I learned this when I was in college. The night before an exam, I would look over the material just before I went to sleep and again before I got out of bed the next morning. Then I would go to class and get an "A" on the exam.

I have used the same principle with the Word of God. When I am memorizing certain books of the Bible, I look at the passage just before I go to sleep. Then the next morning before I do anything else, I get that material into my mind first.

When you wake up, your mind is like a blackboard that has been erased. You should see that the thing which comes first into your spirit and mind is the Word. If you want the Word to be number one in your life, get into it first, before anything else.

Remember, Daniel prayed three times a day. Now I am not advocating limiting prayer to only three times a day. You can pray anytime, and you should. Paul instructs us in 1 Thessalonians 5:17 to *pray without ceasing*. But it is important to have a specific time set aside for prayer.

What happened after Daniel prayed?

Then was the secret revealed unto Daniel in a night vision.

Daniel 2:19

God gave Daniel the answer he sought. He showed him the dream and its interpretation. The next day Daniel went in and told the king what he had dreamed and what it meant. Nebuchadnezzar was so impressed, he said:

Of a truth it is, that your God is a God of gods, and a Lord of kings, and a revealer of secrets, seeing thou couldest reveal this secret.

Daniel 2:47

Nebuchadnezzar had a revelation of the Triune God because of the dream that Daniel interpreted. And Nebuchadnezzar made Daniel a ruler; he gave him a great place in his kingdom. We can see that Daniel was a giant, not a grasshopper. He was a giant because he purposed in his heart, and he prayed regularly.

Step Three: Perception

When Daniel prayed, God did something else: He gave him **perception.** When you purpose and when you pray, you get spiritual perception in the things of God. This is one of the most important things that can happen to us as Christians.

Now, let's look at Shadrach, Meshach, and Abednego. They also had received name changes, but, like Daniel, they were not changed in their hearts or attitudes. Inside, they kept the same spiritual names they had been given at birth: Hananiah, Mishael, and Azariah. For example, *Mishael* means "like God." Mishael chose to receive this as his image of himself, rather than the Chaldean image.

Later on, we read where Nebuchadnezzar demanded all his chiefs to bow down and worship the image he had constructed. When the three Hebrew children refused, the king said to them:

If ye worship not, ye shall be cast the same hour into the midst of a burning fiery furnace; and who is that God that shall deliver you out of my hands?

Daniel 3:15

The three Hebrew children answered:

O Nebuchadnezzar, we are not careful to answer thee in this matter.

If it be so, our God whom we serve is able to deliver us from the burning fiery furnace, and he will deliver us out of thine hand, O king.

But if not, be it known unto thee, O king, that we will not serve thy gods, nor worship the golden image which thou hast set up.

Daniel 3:16-18

These men not only had faith, they had faithfulness. You must have both.

When it appears that your faith has failed, are you going to "hang it up," or are you going to "hang in there"? When you "blow it," are you going to say, "What's the use of trying?" Or will you say, "I'll be faithful, no matter what." Remember, God is developing both things in His children, faith **and** faithfulness.

Of course, we all remember the story. The Hebrew children were delivered by God from the fiery furnace and Nebuchadnezzar was so impressed that he declared:

That every people, nation, and language, which speak any thing amiss against the God of Shadrach, Meshach, and Abednego, shall be cut in pieces, and their houses shall be made a dunghill: because there is no other God that can deliver after this sort.

Daniel 3:29

The only problem was that Nebuchadnezzar ordered respect for Jehovah—the God of Shadrach, Meshach, and Abednego—but he did not make their God his God. Later on, this caused him grief.

The story is told in the fourth chapter of Daniel. This chapter is an actual historical document, written by Nebuchadnezzar himself and found in the historical Persian documents. It tells us that Nebuchadnezzar was a very proud man. He did not see God as the force who made him a giant; he boasted that he had made himself a giant. That is an ego trip. It is God's Word that makes us great. It is Jesus in us Who puts us over, not our self-made man. The self-made man is poorly constructed!

Nebuchadnezzar had another dream, and this time he saw a tree cut down to the ground. Daniel came to him and gave him the interpretation: "If you don't repent, if you don't turn to God, you are going to become like an animal." God gave Nebuchadnezzar one year to repent.

Now, consider the revelations that Nebuchadnezzar had received. After

Daniel interpreted the first dream, Nebuchadnezzar said, "Oh, Daniel, your God is tremendous!" But he would not personally accept Daniel's God. Then he saw the three Hebrew children delivered from the fiery furnace. He saw them become giants because they confessed the Word. But he still would not receive their God. Why not? Because Nebuchadnezzar was his own god.

We see the term *watchers* used several times in this fourth chapter. For example, in verse 13 we read:

I saw in the visions of my head upon my bed, and, behold, a watcher and an holy one came down from heaven.

The watchers in heaven were waiting and watching to see what the king would do. One day he stood up and looked at his empire and said, "Look at this great empire I have built." When he said that, the watchers said, "That's enough!"

The Bible tells us that immediately Nebuchadnezzar was struck with a mental illness. He thought he was an animal and started acting like one. He walked around like a dog; his fingernails grew out like claws; and his hair grew as long as an animal's. (v. 33.) Think how embarrassing it must have been when people came to see the king and were told that he was out in the garden leaping and barking like a dog! (This condition is real; it is called lycanthropy.)

Nebuchadnezzar's son had to take over the throne for him. However, at the end of seven years, the king was restored to his right mind. He tells us about it in his own words:

And at the end of the days I Nebuchadnezzar lifted up mine eyes unto heaven, and mine understanding returned unto me, and I blessed the most High, and I praised and honoured him that liveth for ever, whose dominion is an everlasting dominion, and his kingdom is from generation to generation.

Daniel 4:34

When you see people in the world who have a big self-image, an ego image, you can be sure they will wind up as grasshoppers if they don't get their eyes on God.

Nebuchadnezzar became the lowly one and Daniel stayed the giant. Why? Because Daniel purposed in his heart and prayed. When he prayed, he received spiritual perception because God was big in him.

When you begin to purpose in your heart, when you begin to pray, you are going to receive revelation knowledge. Have you ever heard someone speak and thought to yourself, *Others get so much out of the Word! What's wrong with me? Why don't I get more?* If you have ever felt that way, don't. God is no respecter of persons. He does not love anyone else more than He loves you. The Bible says in Romans 4:17 that God *calleth those things which be not as though they were*—and pretty soon they are!

If you will start saying the Word instead of griping and complaining, you will begin to see things happen in your own life. **Get hooked on God's Book!**

Step Four: Power

Something happened to Daniel. When he held fast to prayer and faith in God's Word, he became a man of **power.** When you begin to perceive the Word, when the Word is really big in you, you begin to move into power, the power of that Word. How much power did Daniel have?

Well, after Nebuchadnezzar had died, his grandson, Belshazzar, who was a poor king, ascended to the throne. One evening he threw a big party for his friends. When his party began to get a little dull, he decided to add a little excitement to it. He remembered all the beautiful articles, including the lovely golden goblets, which had been taken from the Jewish temple when the Babylonians had overrun Jerusalem.

Belshazzar told his guests, ''Let's bring out those Jewish articles and praise the gods of gold and silver and wood and stone." (Dan. 5:1-4.) In so doing, Belshazzar was preparing to become a grasshopper! Only God makes giants, and they are not of gold, silver, wood, or stone. As Belshazzar started to praise these things, a hand suddenly appeared and a finger wrote on the wall:

MENE, MENE, TEKEL, UPHARSIN (Dan. 5:25).

Everyone was frightened! Belshazzar could not understand what those words meant, so he called for Daniel. Daniel told him: "Oh, king, you are weighed in the balances, and found wanting. Your kingdom is divided and given to the Medes and the Persians." (Dan. 5:27,28.)

Now that may have seemed impossible to King Belshazzar because his kingdom seemed so impregnable. But the Medes and the Persians were really very wise. They found a way to enter the well-protected city of Babylon.

The walls of the city were so wide and so thick that thirteen chariots could be driven side by side around the top of the walls. The River Euphrates went under the wall and through the city. The Medes and Persians simply diverted the river miles upstream. That caused the water level around the wall and in the city to fall.

While Belshazzar was having his party, the water level fell low enough that the Medes and the Persians could come in under the city gates. They met together in the center of the city and Belshazzar was killed that very night. The coup was so quick that it was three days before the Babylonians knew that they had been invaded and taken hostage by the enemy.

What happened to Daniel? Remember he was the giant, not the grasshopper. The Medes and the Persians had heard about him, and they said to him, "Daniel, would you be one of our counselors?"

So, Daniel—the man of purpose, the man of prayer, the man of perception—became the man of power. He was made the number one counselor to the Medes and Persians. Was Daniel too old for such a job? No. God's Word will keep you young. It is eternal. You stand on the Word, and it will never let you down. He upholds all things by the Word of His power. (Heb. 1:3.) **Let His Word uphold you!**

When you read the last six chapters of the Book of Daniel, you will see that it is all revelation. One vision after another after another, and they all tie in with Matthew 24 and the Book of Revelation. Daniel was a man of perception and power.

One day as Daniel was praying, he thought about the captivity. He thought, *Our seventy years of captivity are over.* He lived in the Word. He had read Jeremiah's prophecy. He thought, *Our people are supposed to go back to Israel.*

The Bible tells us about King Cyrus who heard these words from Daniel.

Cyrus was a Persian king, and before him was Darius. Daniel was there through both reigns. Josephus, the historian, tells us that Daniel brought the Book of Isaiah to Cyrus.

Daniel said to the king, ''Did you know that your name is in the Bible?''

Cyrus, shocked to say the least, said, ''How can that be?''

Daniel said, ''Your name is here. It was written a hundred and fifty years before you were born. God prophesied about you and said that you were His shepherd, and that He would open the two-leaved gates of brass and the bars of iron.''

And that is exactly the description of the city of Babylon given before it was ever built by God (found in Isaiah 45:1,2).

Daniel continued, ''God said that He would give you this city, which He has done. He wrote your name there so you would understand that you were to let His people return to their homeland.'' Cyrus had been pre-named by God 150 years before his birth! And Cyrus could not sign his name fast enough to free the captives!

How did Daniel have such power with world rulers? Because he purposed to be a giant, and he knew the way to do it. Daniel became a giant through prayer. I don't believe he ever prayed the problem; I think he prayed the promise. He prayed what God's Word says will come to pass, because he was a man of the Word. In everything he used the Word, and the Word was a powerful weapon.

I like the way he began. When he found his purpose, he named it: "I'm not going to be defiled." He announced it, and he stood by it.

Communication of Faith

That the communication of thy faith may become effectual by the acknowledging of every good thing which is in you in Christ Jesus.

Philemon 1:6

The reason I reiterate the same things over and over is because it makes my faith effectual.

You may not feel like a giant today; you may feel like a grasshopper. But start saying that you are a giant. You will begin to energize your faith and put it into activity.

Daniel announced his faith. He did not go around being a silent believer, just "living the life." I know many people say that they just live the life. Don't be chickenhearted. Purpose in your heart to announce your faith. Put your faith into action. Say it with your mouth. You get what you say, so you need to say today, "I am a giant."

It isn't pride to say good things about yourself. You *are* a giant. That's not pride; that's fact! That's who you are according to God's Word.

Say these words out loud right now:

I am not a grasshopper. I am a giant. I am a big giant. I am a conqueror. I put out all the fiery darts of the enemy, because I overcome them with the Word.

4

Overcoming Fear

The major enemy of the Christian is fear. Fear is always the opposite of faith, and faith is always the answer to fear. Faith comes by hearing, and hearing by the Word; so God's Word is the answer to fear. When we take up the sword of the Spirit, which is the Word of God, against fear, we can undo it.

Faith Overcomes Fear

One of the most exciting psalms is not attributed to David, but to King Hezekiah. Before we read it, I want to look at the background of why it was written. It is interesting that, as we read through the Bible chronologically, we find recorded in the book of Samuel some of the psalms David wrote from his own experiences.

When we see why a psalm was written, what the experience of the writer was that brought forth that particular psalm, what he was going through at the time, we can take that psalm and apply it to the same type experience in our own lives. It then becomes a revelation from God to us.

Hezekiah was a very good king. He was the king of Judah, which was the southern kingdom. His name means "Jehovah is strength." Hezekiah had a real problem when an enemy from Assyria named Sennacherib came up against him. *Sennacherib* means "the moon god has increased brothers." In addition to all the other idols he worshiped, Sennacherib also worshiped the moon god. Hezekiah's God was Jehovah, of course. Sennacherib thus represents the forces of the Devil coming against the forces of God.

Assyria, as a nation, had been very, very successful in their military campaigns. Assyria was located northeast of Israel, and east of Syria and Lebanon, around the fertile crescent that is modern-day Iran. They had conquered one nation after another with relative ease. They took Syria and came down into Israel. As they proceeded south, Samaria was right in the middle of their path.

It is easy to remember how Israel is divided. Judea is in the south, Samaria in the middle, and Galilee in the north. All you have to recall is that ''some area'' (Samaria) is in the middle.

So Sennacherib had conquered Samaria, along with Galilee, and was headed right for Judea, Hezekiah's kingdom. When Sennacherib came up against Judah, the things he said about them and their God were terrible! He cursed Jehovah God, insulting Him and His people in every way.

In 2 Kings 18:17-25 you can read the account of his cursing. He boasted,

"What makes you think your God will deliver you? Have the gods of Samaria delivered them?"

Now Jehovah was not the God of the Samaritans. The ten tribes to the north worshiped the golden calf. There was a golden calf in Dan and one in Bethel. So Sennacherib could not say that they were worshiping Jehovah God. Their worship was mixed with idolatry, and those idols had not been able to deliver them.

Sennacherib said, "We've been conquering one nation after another and their gods couldn't deliver them. But if you say unto me, 'We trust in the Lord our God,' ha! That doesn't mean a thing. We're going to overcome you also."

Then Eliakim, Hezekiah's representative, came out and said to the enemy, Sennacherib, who was screaming at them, "Don't speak in Hebrew; speak in Syrian." In other words, he was saying, "Speak in your own language so our people won't

understand these terrible things being
said against them." But Sennacherib
replied, "I'm not going to do that!"
Then he insulted God even more:

*Hath any of the gods of the nations
delivered at all his land out of the hand of the
king of Assyria? Where are the gods . . . ?*
2 Kings 18:33,34

*But the people of Judah did not respond
because Hezekiah had told them not to reply.*

*And it came to pass, when king Hezekiah
heard it, that he rent his clothes, and
covered himself with sackcloth, and went
into the house of the Lord.*
2 Kings 19:1

And while he was in the temple
praying, he sent a message to the
prophet Isaiah.

*And they said unto him (Isaiah), Thus
saith Hezekiah, This day is a day of trouble,
and of rebuke, and blasphemy: for the
children are come to the birth, and there is
not strength to bring forth.*
2 Kings 19:3

Sometimes you may have faith vision, but without the power in the Word to bring it forth. This is why it is so great when you can have Christians who will stand uncompromisingly with you on the Word. They help you see your vision come to pass. This is a marvelous help to see your faith bring forth a miracle.

When Hezekiah turns to Isaiah for help, God uses Isaiah to raise up enough faith to bring forth His Word:

And Isaiah said unto them, Thus shall ye say to your master, Thus saith the Lord, Be not afraid of the words which thou hast heard, with which the servants of the king of Assyria have blasphemed me.

Behold, I will send a blast upon him, and he shall hear a rumour, and shall return to his own land; and I will cause him to fall by the sword in his own land.

2 Kings 19:6,7

So the army of Assyria arrived. Now it is one thing to hear the word of faith, but quite another to look at your bad circumstances. What if you were in a tiny town surrounded by an enemy of perhaps two or three million? You are trying to say, "Okay, I trust in the Lord," but if you kept looking at the size and strength of that army, it would really try your faith! You would keep saying the Word and trying to retain that Word. But when you looked out and saw all those people, it would probably get difficult to "keep the faith."

But then Isaiah comes on the scene again and speaks the Word:

Then Isaiah the son of Amoz sent to Hezekiah, saying, Thus saith the Lord God of Israel, That which thou hast prayed to me against Sennacherib king of Assyria I have heard.

2 Kings 19:20

Isaiah was saying, "Don't worry. You're going to come out of this thing all right." Then he goes on to tell the king:

141

By the way that he came, by the same shall he return, and shall not come into this city, saith the Lord.

> *2 Kings 19:33*

"Sennacherib is going to go back the same way he came. God is going to defend this city," says Isaiah. "The city will not fall."

Now remember this is not just a story. This is history; it actually happened. We are going to see that these people prayed, and they got exactly what they prayed, what they confessed in the psalms. They received their miracle!

This is the key and the answer to fear when you are surrounded with every kind of crazy enemy that the Devil can send against you.

Now let's see how God delivered them:

And it came to pass that night, that the angel of the Lord went out, and smote in the camp of the Assyrians an hundred fourscore and five thousand: and when they arose early in the morning, behold, they were all dead corpses.

2 Kings 19:35

Notice, it only took one angel of the Lord! Early the next morning when Sennacherib's people arose, they looked around and said, "A hundred and eighty-five thousand of our troops didn't get up this morning. What's wrong with them?" They came and told Sennacherib about the great loss. It was so overwhelming! In one night he had lost 185,000 men!

But Sennacherib still had a big army left. He still could have attacked. But just then, the Word tells us, someone came running into the camp and said, "Sennacherib! Sennacherib! Assyria is under attack! There are huge armies coming against Assyria!" This was only a rumor; it was not true. But the Bible says that Sennacherib gathered up the rest of his army and went home to defend his own nation. When he got back to Assyria, he was so frightened that he went in to worship his idols.

And it came to pass, as he was worshipping in the house of Nisroch his god, that Adrammelech and Sharezer his sons smote him with the sword: and they escaped into the land of Armenia. And Esarhaddon his son reigned in his stead.

2 Kings 19:37

Did his moon god help him? No! While he was worshiping his idol, two of his sons came in and stabbed him in the back! That was the end of Sennacherib.

Did God take care of the Israelites? They never fired an arrow. Hezekiah prayed, Isaiah prophesied, and the people stood on the Word of God. God gave them a psalm and they held onto it. God fought their battles and took care of the whole thing.

In the historical account of the death of these 185,000 men, it is recorded that a plague hit the Assyrian army while they were camped outside the walls of

Jerusalem. History also says there was no angel involved, that it was just a superstition. ''It wasn't an angel that hit them,'' historians have concluded. ''It was a plague!''

But if a plague hit the people on one side of the wall, how could the people on the other side of the wall have kept from being striken by the same plague? That is a ridiculous response! Plagues go everywhere once they begin. No, this was no plague. It was an angel of the Lord sent to fight for Judah!

Hezekiah's Psalm of Deliverance

Psalm 46 is a beautiful answer when we are under attack by fear. Written by Hezekiah for his people in the day of trouble, this psalm was composed **before** they won the victory!

You have to speak the Word beforehand; speaking it afterwards is not faith. Anyone can proclaim these things after they have happened, but God expects us to have this kind of testimony **before** we see the victory come to pass.

God is our refuge and strength, a very present help in trouble.

Therefore will not we fear, though the earth be removed, and though the mountains be carried into the midst of the sea;

Though the waters thereof roar and be troubled, though the mountains shake with the swelling thereof. Selah.

There is a river, the streams whereof shall make glad the city of God, the holy place of the tabernacles of the most High.

God is in the midst of her; she shall not be moved: God shall help her, and that right early.

The heathen raged, the kingdoms were moved: he uttered his voice, the earth melted.

Psalm 46:1-6

Think about all it took to handle the natural problems with the earth. All it took to handle the heathen was the

Word that God spoke! That took care of them—not just 185,000, but the entire army of Sennacherib!

The Lord of hosts is with us; the God of Jacob is our refuge. Selah.

Come, behold the works of the Lord, what desolations he hath made in the earth.

He maketh wars to cease unto the end of the earth; he breaketh the bow, and cutteth the spear in sunder; he burneth the chariot in the fire.

Be still, and know that I am God: I will be exalted among the heathen, I will be exalted in the earth.

The Lord of hosts is with us; the God of Jacob is our refuge. Selah.

Psalm 46:7-11

Do you think that Jehovah God was exalted among the Assyrians? Do you think that after this experience they still believed in that silly moon god of Sennacherib, that "moon god that had increased brothers"? I don't think the moon god increased any brothers that day. There was a decrease. God said, *I will be exalted among the heathen.* And He was!

The Lord of Hosts

The Lord of hosts is with us; the God of Jacob is our refuge. This psalm repeats the phrase *the Lord of hosts.* Who are the *hosts* spoken of here? *Hosts* are angelic forces. God, the Lord of hosts, is the Lord of armies of angels.

There are three specific things referred to as "hosts" in the Bible.

The word is first used in Genesis 2:1 to refer to stars: *Thus the heavens and the earth were finished, and all the host of them.*

Isaiah 40:26 says: *Lift up your eyes on high, and behold who hath created these things, that bringeth out their hosts by number: he calleth them all by names by the greatness of his might, for that he is strong in power; not one faileth.*

The second thing that "host" can refer to is angels:

And he said, Hear thou therefore the word of the Lord: I saw the Lord sitting on his throne, and all the host of heaven standing by him on his right hand and on his left.

1 Kings 22:19

And suddenly there was with the angel a multitude of the heavenly host praising God, and saying . . . .

Luke 2:13

Finally, "hosts" can refer to people. Exodus 12:41 speaks of *all the hosts of the Lord* who *went out from the land of Egypt.*

Believers can be "hosts." Psalm 103:21 says, *Bless ye the Lord, all ye his hosts; ye ministers of his, that do his pleasure.*

So "the Lord of hosts" is the Lord of stars, of angels, and of people.

The Lord of the Heavens

If we are in trouble, can God do anything in the stars to help us? Is it scriptural for God to move in heaven for us? Joshua asked God to stop the sun in the valley of Ajalon, and God stopped the forces of heaven when man needed it. (Josh. 10:12-14.) He is the Lord of heaven. He will move heaven for you, when you need it.

Another time Elijah called upon the heavens to close, and it didn't rain for three years. Then when he asked God to open the heavens, it rained. (James 5:17,18.)

Do you remember Deborah and Barak? They went out to fight Sisera and his huge army which was threatening Israel. Sisera was camped on a mountain; Deborah and Barak were opposite him on another mountain, with a valley and a river between them. The Bible says *they fought from heaven; the stars in their courses fought against Sisera* (Judg. 5:20).

That means it rained. Sisera's army had iron chariots. Did you ever try to drive an iron chariot in the mud? Sisera came racing down the hill and hit that dry river bed and it began to rain. Those iron chariots just sunk in the mud! The men jumped out and ran off. God moved the stars in the heavens for Israel.

God is saying to you, "If you need anything, I'll move the stars for you. I'll send a rainstorm, or cause a drought, if necessary." He is the Lord of hosts! Remember how strong and mighty He is before you.

If you have ever been in Duluth, Minnesota, you know that you cannot depend upon the weather there. I always try to go there when they are not having a storm; but it seems that whenever I arrive in that city, I encounter a storm of some kind.

One November, I had conducted a very good meeting and everything went fine until Sunday night. Then a bad storm hit. The next morning when I was to leave for my home in Denver, I could not even see out of my fifth-floor hotel room. It was cloudy and densely foggy outside.

After calling the airport, I was told that no flights were scheduled in or out of Duluth that day because of the fog. Having only three days at home between meetings, I didn't want that time cut short in any way.

At first there was fear in my heart. With a delay of a day or more, I would have only a short time to be with my family before I had to leave again.

Then I thought, *No, the Lord of hosts is with me.* So I went over to the window and I **said**, ''Clouds, lift in the name of Jesus, and lift in one hour!'' I checked my watch and timed it for one hour.

I can hear you saying, ''Marilyn! Do you think you should do things like that?'' Why not? Joshua did. Elijah did. And Elijah is described as a man subject to *like passions as we are* (James 5:17). No place in the Bible does it say these people were perfect; it just says they spoke the Word. It is the Word that is perfect.

After telling the clouds to lift, I waited an hour, then I called the airport again. They said, ''Well, it's strange, but that flight to Denver will be leaving on time.'' I got home when I was supposed to!

You can speak to the elements, and God will move the stars for you. Don't be afraid! He is the God of hosts—and that includes the heavens!

The Lord of Angels

God is also called the Lord of angels. What does that mean to you and me? It took just one angel to kill 185,000 people in Hezekiah's time. Does that mean that angels are behind you and me?

According to Hebrews 1:14, angels are ministering spirits sent to minister to the heirs of salvation—and we are the heirs of salvation!

But how do you get your angels to minister for you? You have to speak the Word or angels cannot minister. You will always see that unless you speak the Word, angels will not move.

Psalm 103:20 states: *Bless the Lord, ye his angels, that excel in strength, that do his commandments, hearkening unto the voice of his word.*

Every born-again Christian has angels surrounding him, but some angels have nothing to do. The person they encamp around grumbles all the time, and angels will not move at grumbles. Angels move at the Word.

It is the Word, and only the Word, that makes your angel a messenger, a ministering spirit. When you begin to speak the Word, your angel will say, "My, my, this Christian keeps me busy all the time!"

What do angels have to do with Jacob? As we have read, verse 7 of Psalm 46 says, *The Lord of hosts is with us; the God of Jacob is our refuge.* Now I know that "hosts" are people and stars and angels, but why tie Jacob into this thing?

Did you ever think that God could have done a better job, that He could have done things differently (better) than He did at times? Have you ever asked God why He put certain things in the places He did? Why did He say *the God of Jacob*? Why not *the God of Israel*? I don't think *the God of Jacob* is always the best advertising, do you? After all, Jacob had a few problems. He was a conniver of the first order, and he did some stealing.

Since Jacob's name was changed to Israel, it looks like God would refer to Himself as *the God of Israel*. For God to call Himself *the God of Jacob* points out one very small but highly important fact: Jacob, in his state, had the Lord of hosts with him. Did Jacob have angels with him *before* he was named Israel?

Remember when the ladder came down from heaven and Jacob saw angels ascending and descending on it? (Gen. 28:12.) Jesus used the same example! (John 1:51.) And Jesus is the way for angels to ascend and descend on you.

So there was Jacob: He had just connived his brother out of everything which was rightfully his as the eldest son, and he was running for his life. That night while he slept, he had an angelic visit. The God of Jacob (the Lord of hosts) and His angels came and visited with Jacob while he was in that state. Some people do not believe that God will visit them when their behavior is bad. But God loves us and comes to our rescue anyway. God transforms people and situations. He is the Lord of hosts.

I have been doing a little study on the parable of the bad seed. (Matt. 13:24-30.) The Gospels say that a man planted a field using good seed. Then it speaks of another man who came in the night while the owner slept and planted bad seed (KJV: *tares*) in with the good. Another word for *tares* is *darnel*.

Now the Devil wants to come into our lives and sow something deceptive, doesn't he? So he sows bad seed— darnel—and when that darnel comes up, it looks just like wheat. In fact, you can't tell the difference between the two until they are grown.

Then the servants came to the master and said, "What shall we do? Shall we pull up the darnel?"

The owner replied, "Oh, no! You're liable to pull up some of the precious wheat also."

God is saying here that He supercedes the laws of nature. Darnel can never be changed into wheat, but bad people can be changed into good. We cannot go around trying to root up everyone whom we do not consider to be Christians; God says that is not our business. At the last minute they might turn into wheat. The separation of wheat from tares is an angelic job, not a human one! God is the God of all the Jacobs of this world. He takes Jacobs and turns them into Israels.

Angels were really involved in Jacob's life. Later on, when he was coming back home with his two wives, his twelve children, and all his entourage, he remembered that when he left home, he wasn't exactly number one on his brother Esau's popularity list. His brother was so angry at him then that he had sworn to kill Jacob.

Now that Jacob must return and face Esau, all he can remember is Esau's anger. So here comes Jacob with all following—flocks, herds, servants, wives, children, maids. When he reaches a place called Mahanaim, he stops.

Mahanaim means "two hosts," or "two camps," or "two bands." There, angels come out to meet him. (His name was still Jacob at this time.) Some of the angels stayed in front of him and some in back. But one stayed around with Jacob and he wrestled with him all night long. (Gen. 32:24.) Angels are again involved! That's the God of Jacob. He sends angels to help him in that state. Why? Because Jacob did speak the Word, even though his character did not always go along with the Word.

There is something very pure about the Word of God. Did you ever confess the Word a great deal and memorize scriptures until you felt the purity of the Word in you? I recall once when I was memorizing the book of James. I had been saying those scriptures so much that suddenly I began to feel the purity and holiness of the Word I was saying.

As you speak the Word, repeat the Word, memorize and meditate on the Word, you begin to become like what you are speaking. That's why *death and life are in the power of the tongue* (Prov. 18:21). When you speak God's Word, the purity of it begins to move in you.

The Lord of People

Jacob had spoken the Word, and the angels were involved with him again and again. Now that is great, but there is something else. The Lord of hosts— the Lord of angels—is also the Lord of people.

So Jacob met Esau. When they met after all that time, what happened?

They embraced and there was peace between them because God is the Lord of people. He can cause people to get behind you instead of against you. Have you ever had favor with people who used to hate you?

I have claimed favor with atheists. When I had a television program called, "The Bible, The Source," some atheists called the station and said, "We're atheists, but we want Marilyn Hickey's program to stay on the air."

Now that is not natural! But it is the work of the Lord of hosts. He is over people, and He can cause people to do what He wants them to do.

Think of how Sennacherib's army went running home over a rumor. Think how the children of Israel got what they said! God is the Lord of hosts, and He will take care of His people. This is a piece of very good news for you in your situation!

The Lord of Stars

How did stars come into Jacob's life? We can see angels and people, but what about stars? God spoke to Jacob and said, "Jacob, I'm going to make your seed like the stars in the heavens." (Ex. 32:13.)

The Lord of Hosts in Control

God is involved in all these areas. That is why He is saying to us, "Don't be afraid." In Psalm 46 you can see three areas or segments in which He says, "Be not afraid." In verses 1-3 He is saying, "Don't be afraid of nature," because He is the Lord of nature. He can move the stars. Then in verses 4-7, when the people come out and attack the city, He is the Lord over people—the Lord of hosts. Then in verses 8-11 there is a warring world. We see that angels are always involved with warring worlds.

As the Lord of hosts, God is over all three areas, and He is saying, "Don't be afraid."

161

Living Water

Now let's look at something else in Psalm 46. Verse 4 says:

There is a river, the streams whereof shall make glad the city of God, the holy place of the tabernacles of the most High.

I know that those people were very concerned with the river. But still, this psalm always ties back with Jacob, and I couldn't quite understand the connection between the river and Jacob. How could they be involved together? Then the Spirit of the Lord led me in my study, and I began to look to see how Jacob was involved with water.

Do you remember the woman at the well in John, chapter 4? What well was it? Jacob's well! When the woman came there, she and Jesus talked a great deal about water. The woman said, ''Our father, Jacob, gave us this well.'' (v. 12.)

I looked up the word for ''well'' in this verse. It is the Greek word *phrear*, which does not mean a well in the sense that the woman spoke of it; it means a cistern, or a place where you catch rainwater. The water is static. It just stands there in the cistern without movement.

In verse 6 the Word says, *Now Jacob's well was there.* In this verse the Greek word translated "well" is *pege,* meaning a fount or fountain.

In verse 14 when Jesus spoke of a well, He used the word *pege,* which refers to a fountain or a spring of water. It is also called "living water" by Jesus. In other words, it is a spring.

Now what does a spring do? Is it static water? No. It is continually fed because it is bubbling up all the time. So Jesus was saying to the woman, "This well isn't static water as you have said; it is bubbling with life." When Jesus speaks about the water "coming up," it is the word for "spring water," and means literally "leaping water."

Jacob had found the Water of Life. When that well is called "Jacob's well," it is not called by the word that the woman used—*static water*—but is called "leaping water," bubbling up.

I think that is what happens to Christians who do not stay in the Word. They become "static." They say, "Oh, I've read the Bible through ten times! I don't need to read it every day. I already know more about it than the pastor knows anyway."

Do you know what that knowledge is? It is accumulated water. Do you like to drink stale, accumulated water? If you leave a glass of water on the bedstand all night long, do you want to drink it the next morning? You usually pour it out and get a fresh glassful to drink, don't you?

The Word of God is not just accumulated water; it is leaping water, springing water. That's why it is so necessary that you be in it every day. You need to get a fresh supply daily so that it bubbles up in your spirit. That's the Word coming alive in you.

The River of Life

In John 7:37,38 we read:

In the last day, that great day of the feast, Jesus stood and cried, saying, If any man thirst, let him come unto me, and drink.

He that believeth on me, as the scripture hath said, out of his belly shall flow rivers of living water.

On the last day of the Feast of Tabernacles, the Bible tells us that Jesus stood up and said, "Out of your belly shall flow rivers of living water." That's leaping water—bubble, bubble, bubble! Every time you see leaping water, you feel like leaping. Sometimes when I get a scripture that is so exciting to me, I want to leap.

The last day, *that great day of the feast*, is the eighth day. What happened on that day is very interesting. For seven days, it was traditional that the priests use golden vessels. They would walk down from the temple, which would have been down into the valley, into what we call Hezekiah's tunnel. That's where they got most of their water. The original tunnel is still there, unchanged.

Remember, this is Hezekiah's tunnel, and Hezekiah wrote this psalm, so he knows about water, and about water in that city. This is the river that supplied the total water supply for the city of Jerusalem, and this tunnel was carved in stone.

The priests would go down there and carry back water in those golden vessels. They would bring it into the temple courtyard. This act was to symbolize what God had done for them in the wilderness.

In the wilderness the children of Israel always had water. One time they had to hit a rock to get it. Another time Moses was supposed to speak to a rock to bring forth water. Another time they were to dig in the sand. (They did not see any water there at all!) The last time they dug in the sand, they had to sing to the sand and say, ''Spring up, O well! Spring up, O well!'' while they were digging. (Num. 21:17.)

Wouldn't you look silly doing that? You know, sometimes saying the Word does make you look silly. But they spoke the Word to the sand, and soon it went bubble, bubble—and up came water!

At the Feast of Tabernacles the Israelites poured out the water they had brought to show how God always gave them water in the wilderness.

"Now He has moved us into the city of Jerusalem," they were saying symbolically, "and we have a river for water." It was not a very big river, true; but it was a river nevertheless.

But on the eighth day they didn't pour out water. The last day of the feast they said, "There's something new coming forth, and it will be more than a well, more than a river." They were thinking of the great outpouring of Joel's prophecy. (Joel 2:28.) They were thinking of the river in Ezekiel 47 that comes out of the city of God. They were thinking of that great river, but they had nothing to symbolize it, so they did nothing on the eighth day.

But on the eighth day, Jesus stood up and said, "Out of your belly shall flow rivers of living water." What was the significance of this statement? What was Jesus saying? These people thought that the river of life was going to come out of a **city,** but Jesus was saying that it was going to come out of **people.**

The Word that becomes life inside you not only begins to give you water, but it gets bigger and bigger until it becomes a river; then it goes out and waters more and more people. That's exactly what Jesus meant. It is the "new thing" that God is doing in our day. (Is. 43:19.)

Eight is always the number of new beginnings. God is pouring out rivers, and they are reaching not just a church, not just a segment of a city, but they are reaching the world.

Making Your Faith Effective

Let me insert something here about Jesus and His way of teaching. You will always see Him doing physical things in conjunction with the lesson He is presenting. When Jesus was teaching, the Bible tells us that He always sat down. But when He was proclaiming something, as a herald, He stood up.

In Genesis 2 when God planted a garden, He sent a river leading out of it. God has always wanted rivers coming out of His people. It is not enough for us to experience the Word; it is as we begin to confess the Word and let the Word go out that we begin to see rivers going into different areas.

Can't you picture Hezekiah and all those people standing up when they heard that Sennacherib was outside, and reading Psalm 46 as a defense against him! If you don't say the Word out loud, your faith will not be effective. You can "believe" it from now until doomsday; but until you speak it, it is not yours. I have noticed that the more I say the Word, the more my heart begins to believe it. I will say it, whether I see it or not, because I have noticed that when I do, my spirit begins to line up with the Word.

These people had to say the psalm out loud because they were looking at that army of Sennacherib outside their walls:

God is our refuge and strength, a very present help in trouble.

Therefore will not we fear, though the earth be removed, and though the mountains be carried into the midst of the sea;

Though the waters thereof roar and be troubled, though the mountains shake with the swelling thereof. Selah.

There is a river, the streams whereof shall make glad the city of God, the holy place of the tabernacles of the most High.

God is in the midst of her; she shall not be moved: God shall help her, and that right early.

The heathen raged, the kingdoms were moved: he uttered his voice, the earth melted.

The Lord of hosts is with us; the God of Jacob is our refuge. Selah.

Come, behold the works of the Lord, what desolations he hath made in the earth. He maketh wars to cease unto the end of the earth; he breaketh the bow, and cutteth the spear in sunder; he burneth the chariot in the fire.

Be still, and know that I am God: I will be exalted among the heathen, I will be exalted in the earth.

The Lord of hosts is with us; the God of Jacob is our refuge. Selah.

Be still here is not meant for Christians, but for sinners. God is saying to them, "Be quiet. Know that I am God."

Our God is a refuge, a strength, and a present help in time of trouble. The Hebrew word for strength, as in "God is our refuge and strength," is *azaz*. It means "a vehement wind." Strength means wind.

What filled the upper room on the day of Pentecost? *Wind.*

What opened the Red Sea? *Wind.*

We have strength in the Spirit. This word also means "heroes, security, defense, refuge, splendor, and praising." It is very important that you praise the Lord. Praise brings strength. A part of our strength is worship.

This word also means "activity in deep water." God has strength for swimming in deep waters, whether literal or figurative waters.

When we say, "The Lord of hosts is our God; the God of Jacob is our refuge—our strength, our help," that does not mean He is just around for sweet Christians. Did you ever meet some Christians who were so sweet they gave you an inferiority complex? This says that He is the God of Jacob, and Jacob surely wasn't known for his sweetness.

Then it states, "The Lord of hosts is with us." Every time fear comes around, I can say, "The Lord of hosts is with me!" You can say it, too! He moves stars, He moves angels, and He moves people. He gave me an example in Hezekiah when He gave him victory by the Spirit. Hezekiah took his example and his inspiration from Jacob. They saw heaven move, they saw angels move, and they saw people move. And *you* can see the same thing happen in *your* life!

Banishing Fear

I want to rebuke fear. Fear is the most hideous thing there is. We get afraid of people. *The fear of man bringeth a snare* (Prov. 29:25). We get afraid of finances, of physical problems, of the future, of what might happen. We are afraid that people won't like us. There are all kinds of fears.

Are you ready to get rid of fear?

Put your hand on your heart and say this:

Satan, I curse you and any fear that you would bring down upon me. You

are the defeated one, and I am the victorious one!

You go around trying to plant bad seed in the earth, and the earth isn't even yours. The Bible says that the earth is the Lord's, and the fullness thereof. You come in to plant something that doesn't even belong to you, and you come in while men are asleep. But I'm not asleep; I'm awake! You're not planting anything in me because I am the Lord's, and He has planted His seed in me. That's good seed; it's the Word of God, and it can't return void.

I resist you in Jesus' name! I curse every attack of fear and every longstanding pattern of fear.

Father, I thank You not only for wells bubbling up in me, but for rivers coming forth from me.

In Jesus' name,
Amen.

Marilyn Hickey is a woman greatly used of God.

Besides being wife, mother, and homemaker, Marilyn shares full-time Christian ministry with her husband, Wallace Hickey, who is the founding pastor of Happy  Church in Denver. Early in their ministry together, Marilyn began to study and literally devour the Word. When God called her to teach, He began to open door after door before her. One home Bible study group began to call itself "Life For Laymen." It was from this small group that the present worldwide outreach of Marilyn Hickey Ministries emerged.

Today Marilyn is answering God's call to awaken the "sleeping giant" of Christian laymen and to reveal the authority of God's Word as a creative power. By teaching the Bible in a simple and practical way, Marilyn is bringing the life of God to people throughout the world.

Her multi-faceted organization includes:

- A 15-minute radio program, heard daily on over 100 stations in the United States as well as several stations overseas.
- A daily 15-minute television program, **The Best Day of Your Life,** broadcast in several cities in the United States.

- A weekly half-hour program seen on Trinity Broadcasting's satellite network.
- A monthly manual for contemporary living, **Time With Him,** which takes the reader through the Bible on a day-to-day basis.
- A combination tape/written-lesson series, **The School of Ministries,** designed to help mature the Christian in his daily walk.

Marilyn has authored over 20 books and booklets, and has produced countless teaching tapes that have been sent out around the world.

She travels to cities all over the United States, hosting seminars and miracle services. Because of her obedience to the Lord, the Word always goes forth in power with signs and wonders following.

For information regarding any phase of Marilyn's ministry, write:

Marilyn Hickey Ministries
P. O. Box 10606
Denver, CO 80210